Gerd Wagner and Mircea Diaconescu
Web Applications with Javascript or Java
De Gruyter Graduate

Also of interest

Web Applications with Javascript or Java
Volume 1: Constraint Validation, Enumerations, Special Datatypes
G. Wagner, M. Diaconescu, 2018
ISBN 978-3-11-049993-3, e-ISBN 978-3-11-049995-7,
e-ISBN (EPUB) 978-3-11-049724-3

Programming in C
X. Zhou, Q. Miao, L. Feng, 2020
Volume 1: Basic Data Structures and Program Statements
ISBN 978-3-11-069117-7, e-ISBN 978-3-11-069232-7,
e-ISBN (EPUB) 978-3-11-069249-5

Volume 2: Composite Data Structures and Modularization
ISBN 978-3-11-069229-7, e-ISBN 978-3-11-069230-3,
e-ISBN (EPUB) 978-3-11-069250-1

Analog and Hybrid Computer Programming
B. Ulmann, 2020
ISBN 978-3-11-066207-8, e-ISBN 978-3-11-066220-7,
e-ISBN (EPUB) 978-3-11-066224-5

Elementary Synchronous Programming
in C++ and Java via algorithms
A. S. Janfada, 2019
ISBN 978-3-11-061549-4, e-ISBN 978-3-11-061648-4,
e-ISBN (EPUB) 978-3-11-061673-6

Machine Learning and Visual Perception
B. Zhang, 2020
ISBN 978-3-11-059553-6, e-ISBN 978-3-11-059556-7,
e-ISBN (EPUB) 978-3-11-059322-8

Gerd Wagner and Mircea Diaconescu

Web Applications with Javascript or Java

Volume 2:
Associations and Class Hierarchies

Authors
Prof. Dr. Gerd Wagner
BTU Cottbus-Senftenberg
Fachgebiet Internettechnologie
Konrad-Wachsmann-Allee 5
03046 Cottbus
wagnerg@b-tu.de

Mircea Diaconescu
dimircea@gmail.com

ISBN 978-3-11-050024-0
e-ISBN (PDF) 978-3-11-050032-5
e-ISBN (EPUB) 978-3-11-049756-4

Library of Congress Control Number: 2020948051

Bibliographic information published by the Deutsche Nationalbibliothek
The Deutsche Nationalbibliothek lists this publication in the Deutsche Nationalbibliografie; detailed bibliographic data are available on the Internet at http://dnb.dnb.de.

© 2021 Walter de Gruyter GmbH, Berlin/Boston
Cover image: monsitj/iStock/thinkstock
Typesetting: Integra Software Services Pvt. Ltd.
Printing and binding: CPI books GmbH, Leck

www.degruyter.com

To Our Families.

Foreword

This two-volume book shows how to design and implement web applications with a model-based engineering approach, using the two most relevant technology platforms for web development: JavaScript and Java. Web apps are designed with the help of information models in the form of UML class diagrams and implemented as:

1. JavaScript front-end apps, using one of the two local storage technologies offered by web browsers;
2. Java back-end apps, using Java Server Faces (JSF) as the user interface technology, the Java Persistence API (JPA) for object-to-storage mapping, and a MySQL/MariaDB database management system.

The focus of the book are general concepts and techniques concerning the fundamental *information management* issues of

1. integrity constraints and data validation,
2. enumerations and enumeration attributes
3. unidirectional and bidirectional associations between object types,
4. subtyping and inheritance in class hierarchies.

The first two issues of this list are discussed in Volume 1 of the book, while the last two issues are discussed in Volume 2.

We assume that the reader is already familiar with HTML and with at least one object-oriented programming language, such as C++, Java, PHP, Python or C#. In addition, we assume that the reader has some familiarity with CSS and JavaScript, and is interested to learn more about programming with JavaScript or Java.

The book can be used

1. in web development courses for students of Computer Science or Information Systems and related disciplines;
2. by JavaScript developers for learning Java;
3. by Java developers for learning JavaScript;
4. by JavaScript and Java (and PHP/Python/C# etc.) developers for learning
   - object-oriented (OO) programming with JavaScript or Java,
   - how to implement basic information management concepts and build complete web apps with plain JavaScript or Java.

The book comes with the complete source code of six example apps that you can run or download from our web server.

https://doi.org/10.1515/9783110500325-202

Contents

Part I: **Associations**

List of Figures

https://doi.org/10.1515/9783110500325-204

List of Tables

https://doi.org/10.1515/9783110500325-205

Part I: **Associations**

The three example apps that we have discussed in Volume 1, the *minimal app*, the *validation app*, and the *enumeration app*, have been limited to managing the data of one object type only. A real app, however, has to manage the data of several object types, which are typically related to each other in various ways. In particular, there may be **associations** and **subtype** (inheritance) relationships between object types. Handling associations and subtype relationships are advanced issues in software application engineering. They are often not sufficiently discussed in text books and not well supported by application development frameworks.

Associations are important elements of information models. Software applications have to implement them in a proper way, especially in their *model* layer within a *model-view-controller* (MVC) architecture. Unfortunately, application development frameworks do often not provide much support for dealing with associations.

There are two important distinctions, which are independent of each other:
1. *Functional* versus *non-functional* ("many-to-many") associations.
2. *Unidirectional* versus *bidirectional* associations.

A functional association corresponds to what is called a *function* in mathematics, while a many-to-many association corresponds to what is called a *relation* in mathematics.

A unidirectional association corresponds to a reference property in OO modeling and programming, while a bidirectional association corresponds to a pair of mutually inverse reference properties.

https://doi.org/10.1515/9783110500325-001

1 Reference Properties and Unidirectional Associations

A property defined for an object type, or class, is called a ***reference property*** if its values are *references* that reference an object of another, or of the same, type. For instance, the class `Committee` shown in Figure 1.1 below has a reference property `chair`, the values of which are references to objects of type `ClubMember`.

An ***association*** between object types classifies relationships between objects of those types. For instance, the association *Committee-**has**-ClubMember-**as-chair***, which is visualized as a connection line in the class diagram shown in Figure 1.2 below, classifies the relationships FinanceCommittee-**has**-PeterMiller-**as-chair**, RecruitmentCommittee-**has**-SusanSmith-**as-chair** and AdvisoryCommittee-**has**-SarahAnderson-**as-chair**, where the objects PeterMiller, SusanSmith and SarahAnderson are of type `ClubMember`, and the objects FinanceCommittee, RecruitmentCommittee and AdvisoryCommittee are of type `Committee`. An association as a set of relationships can be represented as a table like so:

*Committee-**has**-ClubMember-**as**-chair*	
Finance Committee	Peter Miller
Recruitment Committee	Susan Smith
Advisory Committee	Sarah Anderson

Reference properties correspond to a special form of associations, namely to ***unidirectional*** *binary associations*. While a binary association does, in general, not need to be directional, a reference property represents a binary association that is directed from the property's domain class (where it is defined) to its range class.

In general, associations are ***relationship types*** with two or more ***object types*** participating in them. An association between two object types is called ***binary***. In this book we only discuss binary associations. For simplicity, we just say 'association' when we actually mean 'binary association'.

While individual relationships (such as FinanceCommittee-**has**-PeterMiller-**as-chair**) are important information items in business communication and in information systems, associations (such as *Committee-**has**-ClubMember-**as-chair***) are important elements of *information models*. Consequently, software applications have to implement them in a proper way, typically as part of their *model* layer within a *model-view-controller* (MVC) architecture. Unfortunately, many application development frameworks lack the required support for dealing with associations.

https://doi.org/10.1515/9783110500325-002

In mathematics, associations have been formalized in an abstract way as sets of uniform tuples, called *relations*. In *Entity-Relationship (ER)* modeling, which is the classical information modeling approach in information systems and software engineering, objects are called *entities*, and associations are called *relationship types*. The *Unified Modeling Language (UML)* includes the *UML Class Diagram* language for information modeling. In UML, object types are called *classes*, relationship types are called *associations*, and individual relationships are called "links". These three terminologies are summarized in the following table:

Our preferred term(s)	UML	ER Diagrams	Mathematics
object	object	entity	individual
object type (class)	class	entity type	unary relation
relationship	link	relationship	tuple
association (relationship type)	association	relationship type	relation
functional association		one-to-one, many-to-one or one-to-many relationship type	function

We first discuss reference properties, which implicitly represent unidirectional binary associations in an "association-free" class model (a model without any explicit association element).

1.1 References and Reference Properties

A reference can be either *human-readable* or an *internal object reference*. Human-readable references refer to identifiers that are used in human communication, such as the unique names of astronomical bodies, the ISBN of books and the employee numbers of the employees of a company. Internal object references refer to the computer memory addresses of OOP objects, thus providing an efficient mechanism for accessing objects in the main memory of a computer.

Some languages, like SQL and XML, only support human-readable, but not internal references. In SQL, human-readable references are called *foreign keys*, and the identifiers they refer to are called *primary keys*. In XML, human-readable references are called *ID references* and the corresponding attribute type is IDREF.

Objects in an OO program can be referenced either with the help of human-readable references (such as integer codes) or with internal object references, which are preferable for accessing objects efficiently in main memory. Following the XML terminology, we call human-readable references *ID references*. We follow the standard naming convention for ID reference properties where an ID reference property defined in a class A and referencing objects of class B has the name b_id using the suffix _id. When we store persistent objects in the form of records or table rows, we need to convert internal object references, stored in properties like publisher, to ID references, stored in properties like publisher_id. This conversion is performed as part of the serialization of the object by assigning the standard identifier value of the referenced object to the ID reference property of the referencing object.

In OO languages, a property is defined for an object type, or class, which is its *domain*. The values of a property are either *data values* from some datatype, in which case the property is called an ***attribute***, or they are *object references* referencing an object from some class, in which case the property is called a ***reference property***. For instance, the class Committee shown in Figure 1.1 below has an attribute name with range String, and a reference property chair with range ClubMember.

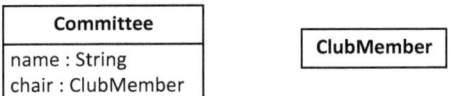

Figure 1.1: A committee has a club member as chair expressed by the reference property chair.

Object-oriented programming languages, such as JavaScript, PHP, Java and C#, directly support the concept of *reference properties*, which are properties whose range is not a *datatype* but a *reference type*, or *class*, and whose values are object references to instances of that class.

By default, the multiplicity of a property is 1, which means that the property is ***mandatory*** and ***functional*** (or, in other words, *single-valued*), having ***exactly one*** value, like the property chair in class Committee shown in Figure 1.1. When a functional property is ***optional*** (not mandatory), it has the multiplicity 0..1, which means that the property's minimum cardinality is 0 and its maximum cardinality is 1.

A reference property can be either ***single-valued*** (*functional*) or ***multi-valued*** (*non-functional*). For instance, the reference property Committee::chair shown in Figure 1.1 is single-valued, since it assigns a unique club member as chair to a club. An example of a *multi-valued* reference property is provided by the property Book::authors shown in Figure 1.11 below.

Normally, the collection value of a multi-valued reference property is a set of references, implying that the order of the references does not matter. In certain cases, however, the order matters and, consequently, the collection value of such a multi-valued reference property is an ordered set of references, typically implemented as a list.

1.2 Referential Integrity

References are important information items in our application's database. However, they are only meaningful, when their *referential integrity* is maintained by the app. This requires that for any reference, there is a referenced object in the database. Consequently, any reference property p with domain class C and range class D comes with a *referential integrity constraint* that has to be checked whenever

1. a new object of type C is created,
2. the value of p is changed for some object of type C,
3. an object of type D is destroyed.

A referential integrity constraint also implies two *change dependencies*:

1. An **object creation dependency**: an object with a reference to another object can only be created after the referenced object has been created.
2. An **object destruction dependency**: an object that is referenced by another object can only be destroyed after
   1. the referencing object is destroyed first (the CASCADE deletion policy), or
   2. the reference in the referencing object is either dropped (the DROP-REFERENCE deletion policy) or replaced by another reference.

   For every reference property in our app's model classes, we have to choose, which of these two possible *deletion policies* applies.

In certain cases, we may want to relax this strict regime and allow creating objects that have non-referencing values for an ID reference property, but we do not consider such cases.

Typically, object creation dependencies are managed in the user interface by not allowing the user to enter a value of an ID reference property, but only to select one from a list of all existing target objects.

1.3 Modeling Reference Properties as Unidirectional Associations

A reference property (such as chair in the example shown in Figure 1.1 above) can be modeled in a UML class diagram in the form of an **association end** owned by its domain class, which is visualized with the help of a small filled circle (also called a "dot"). This requires to connect the domain class and the range class of the reference property with an association line, place an *ownership dot* at the end of this line at the range class side, and annotate this association end with the property name and with a multiplicity symbol, as shown in Figure 1.2 below for the case of our example. In this way we get a **unidirectional association**, the **source** class of which is the property's **domain** and the **target** class of which is the property's **range**.

The fact that an association end is *owned* by the class at the other end, as visually expressed by the *association end ownership dot* at the association end chair in the example shown in Figure 1.2 below, implies that the association end represents a reference property. In the example of Figure 1.2, the represented reference property is Committee::chair having ClubMember as range. Such an association, with only one association end ownership dot, is *unidirectional* in the sense that it allows `navigation´ (object access) in one direction only: from the class at the opposite side of the dot (the *source* class) to the class where the dot is placed (the *target* class).

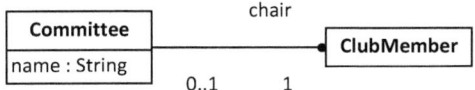

Figure 1.2: An association end with a "dot".

Thus, the two diagrams shown in Figures 1.1 and 1.2 express essentially equivalent models. When a reference property, like chair in Figure 1.1, is modeled by an association end with a "dot", then the property's multiplicity is attached to the association end. Since in a design model, all association ends need to have a multiplicity, we also have to define a multiplicity for the other end at the side of the Committee class, which represents the inverse of the property. This multiplicity (of the inverse property) is not available in the original property description in the model shown in Figure 1.1, so it has to be added according to the intended semantics of the association. It can be obtained by answering the question "is it mandatory that any ClubMember is the chair of a Committee?" for finding the minimum cardinality and the question "can a ClubMember be the chair of more than one Committee?" for finding the maximum cardinality.

When the value of a property is a set of values from its range, the property is **non-functional** and its multiplicity is either 0..* or n..* where n > 0. Instead of 0..*, which means "neither mandatory nor functional", we can simply write the asterisk symbol *. The association shown in Figure 1.2 assigns at most one object of type ClubMember as chair to an object of type Committee. Consequently, it's an example of a **functional association**.

An overview about the different cases of functionality of an association is provided in Table 1.1.

Notice that the directionality and the functionality type of an association are independent of each other. So, a unidirectional association can be either functional (one-to-one or many-to-one), or non-functional (one-to-many or many-to-many).

Table 1.1: Functionality types.

Functionality type	Meaning
one-to-one	both functional and inverse functional
many-to-one	functional
one-to-many	inverse functional
many-to-many	neither functional nor inverse functional

1.4 Representing Unidirectional Associations as Reference Properties

A unidirectional association between a source and a target class can be represented as a reference property of the source class. This is illustrated in Figure 1.3 below for two unidirectional associations: a many-to-one and a many-to-many association.

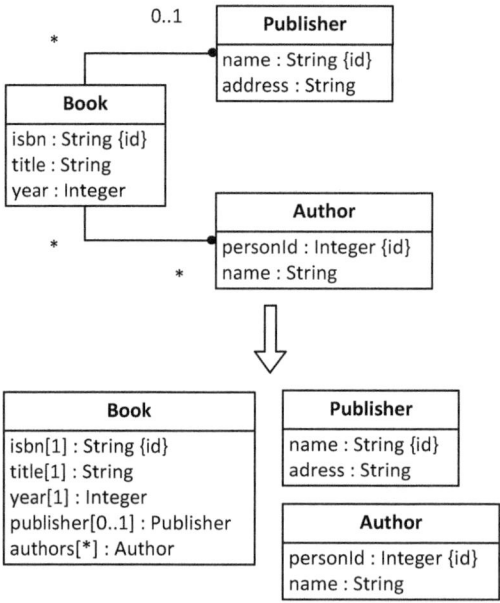

Figure 1.3: Representing unidirectional associations as reference properties.

Notice that, in a way, we have eliminated the two explicit associations and replaced them with corresponding reference properties resulting in a class model that can be coded with a classical OOP language in a straightforward way. OOP languages do not support associations as first class citizens. They do not have a language element for defining associations. Consequently, an OOP class design model, which we call *OO class model*, must not contain any explicit association.

1.5 Adding Directionality to a Non-Directed Association

When we make an information model in the form of a UML class diagram, we typically end up with a model containing one or more associations that do not have any ownership defined for their ends, as, for instance, in Figure 1.4 below. When there is no ownership dot at either end of an association, such as in this example, this means that the model does not specify how the association is to be represented (or realized) with the help of reference properties. Such an association does not have any direction. According to the UML 2.5 specification, the ends of such an association are "owned" by itself, and not by any of the classes participating in it.

Figure 1.4: A model of a non-directed association between Committee and ClubMember.

An information design model that contains an association without association end ownership dots is acceptable as a *relational database* design model, but it is incomplete as a design model for OOP languages.

  For instance, the model of Figure 1.4 provides a relational database design with two entity tables, `committees` and `clubmembers`, and a separate one-to-one relationship table `committee_has_clubmember_as_chair`. But it does not provide a design for Java classes, since it does not specify how the association is to be implemented with the help of reference properties.

  There are three options how to turn an information design model of a non-directed association (without any association end ownership dots) into an information design model where all associations are either unidirectional or bidirectional: we can place an ownership dot at either end or at both ends of the association. Each of these three options defines a different way how to represent, or implement, the association with the help of reference properties. So, for the association shown in Figure 1.4 above, we have the following options:

1. Place an ownership dot at the `chair` association end, leading to the model shown in Figure 1.2 above, which can be transformed into the OO class model shown in Figure 1.1 above.

2. Place an ownership dot at the `chairedCommittee` association end, leading to the completed models shown in Figure 1.8 below.
3. Make the association bidirectional by placing ownership dots at both association ends, as shown in Figure 1.5, with the meaning that the association is implemented in a redundant manner by a pair of mutually inverse reference properties `Committee::chair` and `ClubMember::chairedCommittee`, as discussed in Chapter 7.

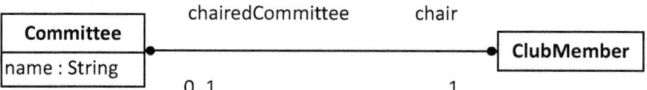

Figure 1.5: Modeling a bidirectional association between Committee and ClubMember.

So, whenever we have modeled an association, we have to make a choice, which of its ends represents a reference property and will therefore be marked with an ownership dot. It can be either one, or both. This decision also implies a decision about the *navigability* of the association. When an association end represents a reference property, this implies that it is navigable (via this property).

In the case of a functional association that is not one-to-one, the simplest design is obtained by defining the direction of the association according to its functionality, placing the association end ownership dot at the association end with the multiplicity `0..1` or `1`. For a non-directed one-to-one or many-to-many association, we can choose the direction as we like, that is, we can place the ownership dot at either association end.

1.6 Our Running Example

The model shown in Figure 1.6 below (about publishers and books) serves as our running example for a unidirectional functional association. Notice that it contains the unidirectional many-to-one association *Book-**has**-Publisher*.

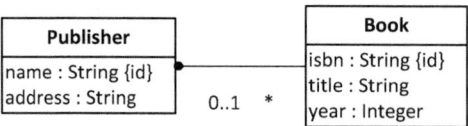

Figure 1.6: The Publisher-Book information design model with a unidirectional association.

We may also have to deal with a non-functional (multi-valued) reference property representing a unidirectional non-functional association. For instance, the unidirectional many-to-many association between Book and Author shown in Figure 1.7 below, models a multi-valued (non-functional) reference property authors.

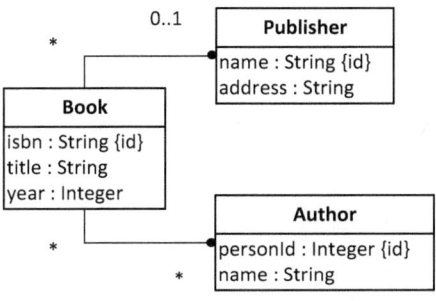

Figure 1.7: The Publisher-Book-Author information design model with two unidirectional associations.

1.7 Eliminating Unidirectional Associations

Since classical OO programming languages do not support associations as first class citizens, but only classes and reference properties representing unidirectional associations, we have to eliminate all explicit associations from general information design models for obtaining OO class models.

1.7.1 The Basic Elimination Procedure

The starting point of our restricted *association elimination* procedure is an information design model with various kinds of unidirectional associations, such as the model shown in Figure 1.6 above. If the model still contains any non-directional associations, we first have to turn them into directional ones by making a decision on the ownership of their ends, as discussed in Section 1.5.

A unidirectional association connecting a source with a target class is replaced with a corresponding reference property in its source class having

1. the same name as the association end, if there is any, otherwise it is set to the name of the target class (possibly pluralized, if the reference property is multi-valued);
2. the target class as its range;
3. the same multiplicity as the target association end,
4. a uniqueness constraint if the unidirectional association is inverse functional.

This replacement procedure is illustrated for the case of a unidirectional one-to-one association in Figure 1.8 below, where the uniqueness constraint of the reference property chairedCommittee is expressed by the {key} property modifier.

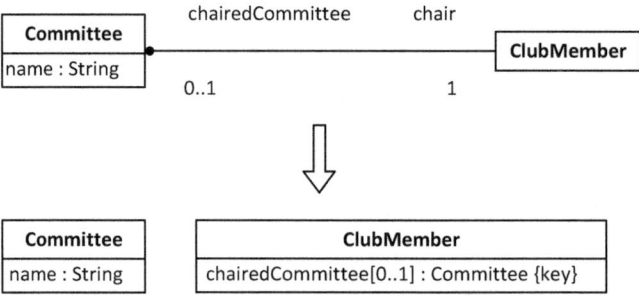

Figure 1.8: Turning a functional association end into a reference property.

For the case of a unidirectional one-to-many association, Figure 1.9 below provides an illustration of the association elimination procedure. Here, the non-functional association end at the target class Point is turned into a corresponding reference property with name points obtained as the pluralized form of the target class name.

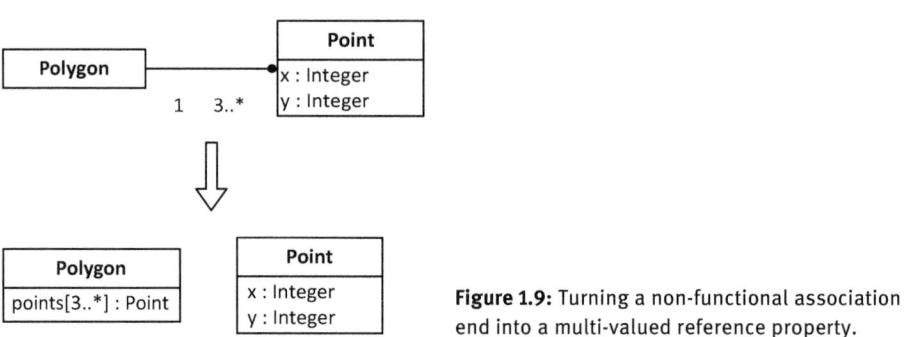

Figure 1.9: Turning a non-functional association end into a multi-valued reference property.

1.7.2 Eliminating Associations from the Design Model

In the case of our running example, the *Publisher-Book-Author* information design model, we have to replace both unidirectional associations with suitable reference properties. In the first step, we replace the many-to-one association *Book-**has**-Publisher* in the model of Figure 1.6 with a functional reference property publisher in the class Book, resulting in the OO class model shown in Figure 1.10:

Book
isbn[1] : String {id}
title[1] : String
year[1] : Integer
publisher[0..1] : Publisher

Publisher
name : String {id}
adress : String

Figure 1.10: An OO class model for Publisher and Book.

Notice that since the target association end of the *Book*-**has**-*Publisher* association has the multiplicity 0..1, we have to declare the new property publisher as optional by defining its multiplicity to be 0..1.

The meaning of this OO class model and its reference property publisher can be illustrated by a sample data population for the two model classes Book and Publisher as presented in the following tables:

Publisher

Name	Address
Bantam Books	New York, USA
Basic Books	New York, USA

Book

ISBN	Title	Year	Publisher
0553345842	The Mind's I	1982	Bantam Books
1463794762	The Critique of Pure Reason	2011	
1928565379	The Critique of Practical Reason	2009	
0465030793	I Am A Strange Loop	2000	Basic Books

Notice that the values of the "Publisher" column of the *Book* table are unique names that reference a row of the *Publisher* table. The "Publisher" column may not have a value for certain rows due to the fact that the corresponding reference property publisher is optional.

In the second step, we replace the many-to-many association *Book*-**has**-*Author* in the model of Figure 1.7 with a multi-valued reference property authors in the class Book, resulting in the OO class model shown in Figure 1.11.

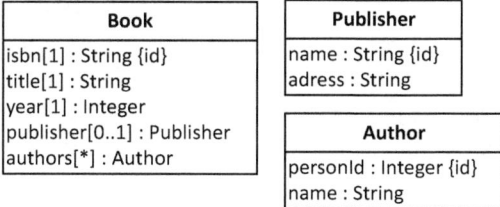

Figure 1.11: An OO class model for the classes Book, Publisher and Author.

The meaning of this OO class model and its reference properties Book::publisher and Book::authors can be illustrated by sample data populations for the three model classes:

Publisher

Name	Address
Bantam Books	New York, USA
Basic Books	New York, USA

Book

ISBN	Title	Year	Authors	Publisher
0553345842	The Mind's I	1982	1, 2	Bantam Books
1463794762	The Critique of Pure Reason	2011	3	
1928565379	The Critique of Practical Reason	2009	3	
0465030793	I Am A Strange Loop	2000	2	Basic Books

Author

Author ID	Name
1	Daniel Dennett
2	Douglas Hofstadter
3	Immanuel Kant

After the platform-independent OO class model has been completed, one or more platform-specific implementation models, for a choice of specific implementation platforms, can be derived from it. Examples of types of platform-specific implementation models are *JS class models*, *Java Entity class models* and *SQL table models*.

A platform-specific implementation model can still be expressed in the form of a UML class diagram, but it contains only modeling elements that can be directly coded in the chosen platform. Thus, for any platform considered, two guidelines are needed: 1) how to make the platform-specific implementation model, and 2) how to code this model.

1.8 Rendering Reference Properties in the User Interface

The widgets used for data input and output in a (CRUD) data management user interface (UI) normally correspond to properties defined in a model class of an app. We have to distinguish between (various types of) *input fields* corresponding to (various kinds of) *attributes*, and *choice widgets* (such as *selection lists*) corresponding to *enumeration attributes* or to *reference properties*. Representing reference properties in the UI with select controls, instead of input fields, prevents the user from entering invalid ID references, so it takes care of *referential integrity*.

In general, a **single-valued reference property** can be rendered as a single-selection list in the UI, no matter how many objects populate the reference property's range, from which one specific choice is to be made. If the cardinality of the reference property's range is sufficiently small (say, not greater than 7), then we can also use a *radio button group* instead of a selection list.

A **multi-valued reference property** can be rendered as a multiple-selection list in the UI. However, the corresponding multiple-select control of HTML is not really usable as soon as there are many (say, more than 20) different options to choose from because the way it renders the choice is visually too scattered. In the special case of having only a few (say, no more than 7) options, we can also use a checkbox group instead of a multiple-selection list. But for the general case of having in the UI a list containing all associated objects chosen from the reference property's range class, we need to develop a special UI widget that allows to add (and remove) objects to (and from) a list of chosen objects.

Such a **multiple-choice widget** consists of
1. an HTML list element containing the chosen (associated) objects, where each list item contains a push button for removing the object from the choice;
2. a single-select control that, in combination with a push button, allows to add a new associated object from the range of the multi-valued reference property.

1.9 Collection Types for Multi-Valued Reference Properties

By default, a non-functional association end associates a **set** of instances of the target class to any instance of the source class, which means that the collection values of the corresponding multi-valued reference property are sets. However, there are also cases, where a non-functional association end is **ordered** and, consequently, the collection values of the corresponding multi-valued reference property take the form of **ordered sets**.

In the following example, the association end publishedBooks is not ordered, while the association end authors is ordered since the order of the authors of a book is meaningful. Notice that in a UML class diagram, an ordered association end is marked up with the annotation {ordered}.

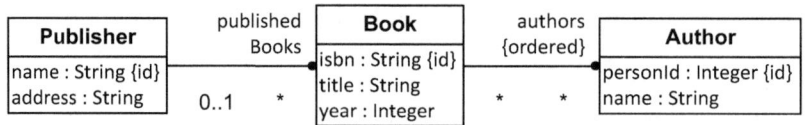

An ordered association end should not represent any ordering based on the properties of the target class. In our example, this implies that the ordering of the authors of a book should, for example, not represent their alphabetical ordering, but rather it should represent information that is not available via the properties of Author. This is, indeed, the case, since it represents some sort of significance, which is not expressed by any property.

Notice that ordered association ends in information design models are just a convenience feature, because an ordered association end can always be transformed into an unordered one by adding one or more attributes to the association's target class, such that these attributes' values can be used for the ordering. Ordered association ends allow a more concise information model, and a more efficient implementation, by not requiring to make the ordering information explicit with the help of auxiliary ordering attributes.

The two important types of collections for multi-valued reference properties are *sets* and *ordered sets*, while use cases for *bags* (multi-sets) and *sequences* (ordered multi-sets) as the collection type of a multi-valued reference property are rare. When the collection type of a multi-valued reference property is bag (or sequence), this can be expressed in the class diagram with the help of the annotation {nonunique} (or {ordered, nonunique}) in the annotation of the association end or property modifier.

Notice, however, that it is quite common to use *lists* (such as JS arrays or the Java interface type List) as the range of multi-valued reference properties, both for ordered and for unordered properties.

1.10 Quiz Questions

If you would like to look up the answers for the following quiz questions, you can check our discussion forum. If you don't find an answer in the forum, you may create a post asking for an answer to a particular question.

1.10.1 Question 1: Meaning of "one-to-one"

What does it mean to say that an association is "one-to-one"?
It means that it is (select one):
1. O Bidirectional
2. O Both functional and total
3. O Functional
4. O Both functional and inverse functional

1.10.2 Question 2: When to Check Referential Integrity

A referential integrity constraint for a reference property p with domain class C and range class D has to be checked whenever (select one or many):
1. ☐ An object of type C is destroyed.
2. ☐ The value of p is changed for some object of type C.
3. ☐ A new object of type C is created.
4. ☐ An object of type D is destroyed.
5. ☐ A new object of type D is created.

1.10.3 Question 3: Meaning of "Functional"

A unidirectional binary association is functional if and only if (select one):
1. O Each object of the source class is linked to at most one object of the target class.
2. O Each object of the target class is linked to at most one object of the source class.
3. O Each object of the source class is linked to at least one object of the target class.
4. O Each object of the source class is linked to exactly one object of the target class.

1.10.4 Question 4: Object Destruction Dependency

Assume that we have an object type B with a standard identifier attribute id and an object type A with an ID reference attribute b_id referencing B::id. Further, assume that there is an object b of type B with b.id = 11 and an object a of type A referencing b with a.b_id = 11. Which of the following statements are correct? Select one or many:
1. ☐ The object b can be destroyed when the ID reference in object a is unassigned (by setting a.b_id to undefined in JS or to null in Java) and there is no other object that references b.
2. ☐ The object a can only be destroyed when b has been destroyed before.

3. □ The object b can be destroyed when the ID reference in object a is reset to another object of type B, e.g. by setting a.b_id = 7 and there is no other object that references b.
4. □ The object b can be destroyed when a has been destroyed before.

1.10.5 Question 5: Rendering a Single-Valued Reference Property

Which of the following statements about a ***single-valued*** *reference property p* and how it should be rendered in a web user interface by a suitable form control are correct? Select one or many:

1. □ An adequate rendering is obtained by using an input control with type="text".
2. □ If the cardinality of *p*'s range is not greater than 7, it can be rendered by a *check button group*.
3. □ If the cardinality of *p*'s range is not greater than 7, it can be rendered by a *radio button group*.
4. □ It can always be rendered by a single-select control.

1.10.6 Question 6: Expressing a Functionality Type

Which term of the form "x-to-y" (where x,y denote "one" or "many") can be used for expressing that an association is neither functional nor inverse functional?

Answer: _____

2 Implementing Unidirectional Functional Associations with Plain JS

A unidirectional *functional* association is either one-to-one or many-to-one. In both cases such an association is represented, or implemented, with the help of a *single-valued* reference property.

In this chapter, we show
1. how to derive a plain JS class model from an OO class model with single-valued reference properties representing *unidirectional functional associations*,
2. how to code the JS class model in the form of plain JavaScript model classes,
3. how to write the view and controller code based on the model code.

Before we show how to derive a plain JS class model and code it in JavaScript, we first introduce a few new elements of the JavaScript language, which we are going to use throughout the JavaScript code discussed in this book.

2.1 New JavaScript Elements

In this section, we present the most important new language elements introduced to JavaScript by ECMAScript 2015+ (that is, 2015+16+17+18+19+20+ . . .).

2.1.1 Block-Scope Variable Declarations with let and const

ES5 did not allow declaring variables the scope of which is a block delimited by a pair of curly braces, { and }, or defined by a for loop. Rather, all variables declared with var, even if declared within a block, have either a function scope or the global scope. The new feature of *block-scope variable declarations* with **let** and **const** allows declaring local variables with a finer-grained scope, which helps avoiding unintended variable duplications and leads to more modular code.

There is only one meaning difference between let and const. Variables declared with const are *frozen* or *immutable*, and in this sense *constant*, while let variables are not. It is preferable to use const for all variables that are not supposed to change their values. Otherwise, or if this is not clear, one should declare the variable with let if it is a block-scoped variable, or with var if it is a global or function-scoped variable.

https://doi.org/10.1515/9783110500325-003

2.1.2 Arrow Functions

Compared to classical JS functions, arrow functions (with =>) provide a more concise function expression syntax, see Ex. 1, and allow using JavaScript's this variable from the function's outer environment (its *closure*) in their function body, see Ex. 2.

Example 2.1.
```
let evens = [0,2,4,6,8];
let odds = evens.map( v => v+1); // [1,3,5,7,9]
// instead of evens.map( function (v) {return v+1;})
```

Example 2.2.
```
this.nums = [1,3,5,8,10,12,15,17];
this.fives = [];
this.nums.forEach( v => {if (v % 5 === 0) this.fives.push(v);});
// instead of this.nums.forEach(
//    function (v) {if (v % 5 === 0) this.fives.push(v);}, this)
```

2.1.3 For-Of Loops over Iterable Objects

Iterable objects include strings, arrays, array-like objects (e.g., the built-in arguments object or instances of HTMLCollections and NodeList), and instances of the datatype objects TypedArray, Map, and Set, as well as user-defined iterables. For instance,

```
const divElems = document.getElementsByTagName("div");
// an HTMLCollection is iterable
for (let dEl of divElems) {
   console.log( dEl.id);
}
```

A *for-of* loop is often more handy than a *for* loop whenever a counter variable is not needed. As opposed to a forEach loop, a *for-of* loop allows iterating over HTMLCollections and can be abandoned with break.

2.1.4 Template Literals

. . . are enclosed by backtick characters (like ` . . . `) instead of double or single quotes and allow a concise syntax for (possibly multi-line) string values resulting from a combination of fixed text parts and variables/expressions. For instance,

```
const classValues = "card important";
const name = "Joker";
const htmlTemplate = `<div class="${classValues}">
  <p>Hello ${name}!</p>
</div>`
```

2.1.5 The Spread Operator

. . . allows spreading (1) the elements of an iterable collection in places where arguments for function calls or array elements are expected, or (2) the slots of a JS object in places where name-value pairs are expected. For instance,

```
let nums = [3,4,5], otherNums = [1, 2, . . . nums]; // [1,2,3,4,5]
// cloning an array
let numsClone = [ . . . nums];
// cloning an object
let book = {title:"JavaScript: The Good Parts"};
let bookClone = { . . . book};
```

2.1.6 Destructuring Assignments

. . . allow a concise syntax for assigning the property values of a JS object or the elements of a JS array to corresponding variables. For instance,

```
var point1 = [10,5];
var [x,y] = point1; // a destructuring assignment
console.log(`x = ${x} | y = ${y}`); // x = 10 | y = 5

var person1 = {firstName:"James", lastName:"Bond"};
var {first, last} = person1;
console.log(`first:${first} | last:${last}`);
// Output: first:James | last:Bond
```

Example 2.3. Dealing with multiple return values of a function
```
function getRectangle () {
  return {width: 50, height: 20};
}
const {a, b} = getRectangle();
drawRectangle( a, b);
```

Example 2.4. Swapping two variables
```
var a = 1, b = 2;
[a,b] = [b,a];
console.log(`a = ${a} | b = ${b}`);
// Output: a = 2 | b = 1
```

Example 2.5. Cloning arrays
```
const list = ['red', 'orange', 'yellow'];
const [. . .listClone] = list;
```

Example 2.6. Simplifying functions with parameter records
A function parameter record allows using named arguments in funcction calls instead of argument lists like so:

```
function displayName( paramRec) {
    alert( paramRec.first + " " +    paramRec.last);
};
displayName({first:"James", last:"Bond"});
```

Using Destructuring, the parameter record fields are assigned to ordinary function parameters, simplifying the function's code:

```
function displayName({first, last}) {
    alert( first + " " + last);
}
displayName({first:"James", last:"Bond"});
```

2.2 Implementing Single-Valued Reference Properties

When coding a class, the ES2015 feature of *function parameter destructuring* allows using a single constructor parameter that is a record with a simplified syntax for defining its fields. We make use of this new feature for obtaining a simplified class definition syntax illustrated by the following example:

```
class Book {
    constructor ({isbn, title, year, . . .}) {
        this.isbn = isbn;
        this.title = title;
```

```
    this.year = year;
    . . .
  }
  . . .
}
```

A single-valued reference property, such as the property `publisher` of the object type `Book`, allows storing internal references to objects of another type, such as `Publisher`. When creating a new object, the constructor function needs to have a parameter for allowing to assign a suitable value to the reference property. In a typed programming language, such as Java, we would have to take a decision if this value is expected to be an (internal) object reference or an (external) ID reference. In JavaScript, however, we can take a more flexible approach and allow using either of them, as shown in the following example:

```
class Book {
  constructor ({isbn, title, year,
      publisher, publisher_id}) {
    . . .
    // assign object reference or ID reference
    if (publisher || publisher_id) {
      this.publisher = publisher || publisher_id;
    }
    . . .
  }
  . . .
}
```

Notice that the record parameter's `publisher` field represents a JS object reference while its `publisher_id` field represents an ID reference. In JavaScript, we can use a disjunctive expression like `expr1 || expr2` for getting the value of the first expression, if it is defined (and not 0), or else the value of the second expression. We handle the resulting ambiguity in the property setter by checking the type of the argument as shown in the following code fragment:

```
set publisher(p) {
  var publisher_id = "";
  // p can be an ID reference or an object reference
  publisher_id = (typeof p !== "object") ? p : p.name;
  . . .
  this._publisher = Publisher.instances[ publisher_id];
  . . .
}
```

Notice that the name of a publisher is used as an ID reference, since it is the standard ID of the Publisher class.

2.3 Make a JS Class Model

The starting point for making a JS class model is an OO class model like the one shown in Figure 1.10.

We now show how to derive a JS class model from this OO class model in four steps. For each class in the OO class model:

1. Add a «get/set» stereotype to all (non-derived) single-valued properties, implying that they have implicit getters and setters. Recall that in the setter, the corresponding check operation is invoked and the property is only set, if the check does not detect any constraint violation.

2. Create a **check** operation for each (non-derived) property in order to have a central place for implementing ***property constraints***. For a standard ID attribute (such as Book::isbn), two or three check operations are needed:

   1. A basic check operation, like checkIsbn, for checking all syntactic constraints, but not the *mandatory value* and the *uniqueness* constraints.

   2. A standard ID check operation, like checkIsbnAsId, for checking the *mandatory value* and *uniqueness* constraints that are implied by a standard ID attribute.

   3. If other classes have a reference property that references the class under consideration, add an *ID reference* check operation for checking the *referential integrity* constraint imposed on *ID reference* (or *foreign key*) attributes. For instance, since the Book::publisher property references Publisher objects, we need a checkNameAsIdRef operation in the Publisher class.

For a reference property, such as Book::publisher, the check operation, Book.checkPublisher, has to check the implied *referential integrity constraint* by invoking Publisher.checkNameAsIdRef, and possibly also a *mandatory value constraint*, if the property is mandatory.

3. Add an object serialization function toString() for showing an object's state in error messages and log messages.

4. Add an object-to-storage conversion function toRecord() that prepares a model object for being stored as a row in an entity table, which can be serialized to a JSON string with JSON.stringify such that it can be stored as a value of a key in an app's localStorage datastore.

This leads to the following JS class model for Book, where the class-level ('static') methods are shown underlined:

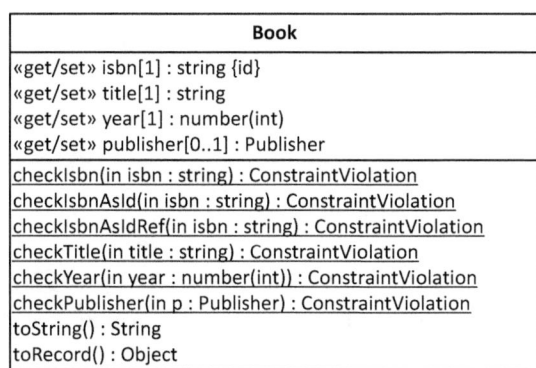

We have to perform a similar transformation also for the class Publisher. This gives us the complete JS class model derived from the above OO class model, as depicted in Figure 2.1.

Book
«get/set» isbn[1] : string {id}
«get/set» title[1] : string
«get/set» year[1] : number(int)
«get/set» publisher[0..1] : Publisher
checkIsbn(in isbn : string) : ConstraintViolation
checkIsbnAsId(in isbn : string) : ConstraintViolation
checkIsbnAsIdRef(in isbn : string) : ConstraintViolation
checkTitle(in title : string) : ConstraintViolation
checkYear(in year : number(int)) : ConstraintViolation
checkPublisher(in p : Publisher) : ConstraintViolation
toString() : String
toRecord() : Object

Publisher
«get/set» name : string {id}
«get/set» adress : string
checkName(in n : string) : ConstraintViolation
checkNameAsId(in n : string) : ConstraintViolation
checkNameAsIdRef(in n : string) : ConstraintViolation
checkAddress(in a : string) : ConstraintViolation
toString() : string
toRecord() : Object

Figure 2.1: A JS class model defining the classes Book and Publisher.

2.4 New Issues

Compared to the validation and enumeration apps discussed in Volume 1, we have to deal with a number of new technical issues:

1. In the *model* code we now have to take care of **reference properties** that require
    1. maintaining **referential integrity**;
    2. choosing and implementing one of the two possible deletion policies discussed in Section 1.2 for managing the corresponding object destruction dependency in the destroy method of the property's range class;
    3. conversion between internal object references and external ID references in the serialization function toString() and the conversion function toRecord(), as well as in the constructor function.
2. In the *user interface ("view")* code we now have to take care of
    1. showing information about associated objects in the *Retrieve/List* use case;
    2. allowing to select an object from a list of all existing instances of the association's target class and add it to, or remove an object from, a list of associated objects, in the *Create* and *Update* use cases.

2.5 Code the Model

The JS class model can be directly coded for getting the JS classes of our app.

2.5.1 Summary

Code each class of the JS class model as an ES2015 class with implicit getters and setters:

1. Code the property checks in the form of class-level ('static') methods. Take care that all constraints of a property as specified in the JS class model are properly coded in the property checks.
2. For each single-valued property, code the specified getter and setter such that in each setter, the corresponding property check is invoked and the property is only set/unset, if the check does not detect any constraint violation.
3. Write the code of the serialization function toString() and the storage conversion function toRecord().
4. Take care of deletion dependencies in the destroy method.

These steps are discussed in more detail in the following sections.

2.5.2 Code Each Model Class as an ES2015 Class

Each class C of the JS class model is coded as an ES2015 class with the same name C
and a constructor having a single record parameter, which specifies a field for each
(non-derived) property of the class. The range of these properties should be indicated in a comment. In the case of a reference property the range is another model
class.

In the constructor body, we assign the fields of the record parameter to corresponding properties. These property assignments invoke the corresponding *setter*
methods.

For instance, the Publisher class from the JS class model is coded in the following way:

```
class Publisher {
  constructor ({name, address}) {
    this.name = name;
    this.address = address;
  }
  . . .
};
```

Since the setters may throw constraint violation exceptions, the constructor function, and any setter, should be called in a try-catch block where the catch clause
takes care of logging suitable error messages.

For each model class C, we define a class-level property C.instances representing the collection of all C instances managed by the application in the form of an
entity table (a map of records). This property is initially set to {}. For instance, in
the case of the model class Publisher, we define:

```
Publisher.instances = {};
```

The Book class from the JS class model is coded in a similar way:

```
class Book {
  constructor ({isbn, title, year, authors, authorIdRefs,
    publisher, publisher_id}) {
  this.isbn = isbn;
  this.title = title;
  this.year = year;
  this.authors = authors || authorIdRefs;
```

```
    if (publisher || publisher_id) {
      this.publisher = publisher || publisher_id;
    }
  }
  . . .
}
```

Notice that the `Book` constructor can be invoked either with object references au-thors and `publisher` or with ID references `authorIdRefs` and `publisher_id`. This approach makes using the `Book` constructor more flexible and more robust.

2.5.3 Code the Property Checks

Take care that all constraints of a property as specified in the JS class model are properly coded in its check function, as explained in Chapter 8 of Volume 1. Recall that constraint violation (or validation error) classes are defined in the file `lib/errorTypes.js`.

For instance, for the `Publisher.checkName` function we obtain the following code:

```
class Publisher {
  . . .
  static checkName(n) {
    if (n === undefined) {
      return new NoConstraintViolation(); // not mandatory
    } else {
      if (typeof n !== "string" || n.trim() === "") {
        return new RangeConstraintViolation (
      "The name must be a non-empty string!"   );
      } else {
        return new NoConstraintViolation();
      }
    }
  }
  static checkNameAsId(n) {. . .}
  . . .
}
```

Notice that, since the name attribute is the standard ID attribute of Publisher, we only check syntactic constraints in checkName, and check the mandatory value and uniqueness constraints in checkNameAsId, which invokes checkName:

```
static checkNameAsId ( n ) {
  var validationResult = Publisher.checkName(n);
  if ((validationResult instanceof NoConstraintViolation)) {
    if (n === undefined) {
      return new MandatoryValueConstraintViolation (
        "A publisher name is required!");
    } else if (Publisher.instances[n]) {
      validationResult = new UniquenessConstraintViolation (
        "There is already a publisher record with this name!");
    } else {
      validationResult = new NoConstraintViolation();
    }
  }
}
```

If we have to deal with ID references (foreign keys) in other classes, we need to provide a further check function, called checkNameAsIdRef, for checking the referential integrity constraint:

```
static checkNameAsIdRef(n) {
  var validationResult = Publisher.checkName(n);
  if ((validationResult instanceof NoConstraintViolation) &&
      n !== undefined) {
    if (!Publisher.instances [n]) {
      validationResult = new ReferentialIntegrityConstraintViolation (
        "There is no publisher record with this name!");
    }
  }
  return validationResult;
}
```

The condition !Publisher.instances[n] checks if there is no publisher object with the given name n, and then creates a validationResult object as an instance of the exception class *ReferentialIntegrityConstraintViolation*. The Book.checkNameAsIdRef function is called by the Book.checkPublisher function:

```
class Book {
    . . .
    static checkPublisher( publisher_id) {
        var validationResult = null;
        if (publisher_id === undefined || publisher_id === "") {
            validationResult = new NoConstraintViolation(); // optional
        } else {
            // invoke foreign key constraint check
            validationResult = Publisher.checkNameAsIdRef( publisher_id);
        }
        return validationResult;
    }
    . . .
}
```

2.5.4 Code the Property Setters

In the setters, the corresponding check function is called and the property is only set, if the check does not detect any constraint violation. In the case of a reference property, we allow invoking the setter either with an object reference or with an ID reference. The resulting ambiguity is resolved by testing if the argument provided in the invocation of the setter is an object or not. For instance, the publisher setter is coded in the following way:

```
class Book {
    . . .
    set publisher( p) {
        if (!p) { // unset publisher
            delete this._publisher;
        } else {
            // p can be an ID reference or an object reference
            const publisher_id = (typeof p !== "object") ? p : p.name;
            const validationResult = Book.checkPublisher( publisher_id);
            if (validationResult instanceof NoConstraintViolation) {
                // create the new publisher reference
                this._publisher = Publisher.instances[ publisher_id];
```

```
      } else {
        throw validationResult;
      }
    }
  }
  . . .
}
```

2.5.5 Choose and Implement a Deletion Policy

For any reference property, we have to choose and implement one of the two possible deletion policies discussed in Section 1.2 for managing the corresponding object destruction dependency in the destroy method of the property's range class. In our case, when deleting a publisher record, we have to choose between

1. deleting all records of books published by the deleted publisher (*Existential Dependency*);
2. dropping from all books published by the deleted publisher the reference to the deleted publisher (*Existential Independence*).

Assuming that books do not existentially depend on their publishers, we choose the second option. This is shown in the following code of the Publisher.destroy method where for all concerned book objects the property book.publisher is cleared:

```
Publisher.destroy = function (name) {
    const publisher = Publisher.instances[name];
    //delete all references to this publisher in book objects
    for (let key of Object.keys( Book.instances)) {
      const book = Book.instances[key];
      if (book.publisher === publisher) {
        delete book._publisher; // delete the slot
        console.log("Book " + book.isbn + " updated.");
      }
    }
    // delete the publisher record
    delete Publisher.instances[name];
    console.log("Publisher " + name + " deleted.");
};
```

Notice that the deletion of all references to the deleted publisher is performed in a sequential scan through all book objects, which may be inefficient when there are many of them. It would be much more efficient when each publisher object would hold a list of references to all books published by this publisher. Creating and maintaining such a list would make the association between books and their publisher *bidirectional*.

2.5.6 Serialization and Object-to-Storage Mapping

In the case of a reference property, like Book::publisher, the serialization function Book::toString() has to show a human-readable identifier of the referenced object, like this.publisher.name:

```
toString() {
  var bookStr = `Book{ ISBN: ${this.isbn}, title: ${this.title},` +
    `year: ${this.year}`;
  if (this.publisher) bookStr += `, publisher: ${this.publisher.name}`;
  return bookStr + "}";
}
```

The object-to-storage conversion function Book::toRecord() converts typed JS objects with object references to corresponding (untyped) record objects with ID references:

```
toRecord() {
  var rec = {};
  for (let p of Object.keys( this)) {
    // copy only property slots with underscore prefix
    if (p.charAt(0) === "_") {
      switch (p) {
      case "_publisher":
        // convert object reference to ID reference
        if (this._publisher) rec.publisher_id = this._publisher.name;
        break;
      default:
        // remove underscore prefix
        rec[p.substr(1)] = this[p];
      }
    }
  };
  return rec;
}
```

The inverse conversion, from untyped record objects with ID references to corresponding typed objects with object references, is performed by the Book constructor, which tolerates both ID references and object references as arguments for setting reference properties.

2.6 Code the View and Controller

The user interface (UI) consists of a start page index.html that allows navigating to data management UI pages, one for each object type (in our example, books.html and publishers.html). Each of these data management UI pages contains 5 sections: a *Manage* section, like *Manage books*, with a menu for choosing a CRUD use case, and a section for each CRUD use case, like *Retrieve/list all books*, *Create book*, *Update book* and *Delete book*, such that only one of them is displayed at any time (for instance, by setting the CSS property display:none for all others).

2.6.1 Initialize the App

For initializing a data management use case, the required data (for instance, all publisher and book records) have to be loaded from persistent storage. This is performed in a controller procedure such as pl.c.books.manage.initialize in c/books.js with the following code:

```
pl.c.books.manage =  {
  initialize: function () {
    Publisher.retrieveAll();
    Book.retrieveAll();
    pl.v.books.manage.setUpUserInterface ();
  }
};
```

The initialize method for managing book data first loads the publishers table and the books table since the book data management UI needs to show their data. Then the book data management menu is rendered by calling the setUpUserInterface procedure.

2.6.2 Showing Associated Objects in *Retrieve/List All*

In our example, we have only one reference property, Book::publisher, which is functional and optional. For showing information about the optional publisher of a book in the *Retrieve/list all* use case, the corresponding cell in the HTML table is filled with the name of the publisher, if there is any:

```
pl.v.books.retrieveAndListAll = {
  setupUserInterface: function () {
    const tableBodyEl = document.querySelector(
            "section#Book-R>table>tbody");
    tableBodyEl.innerHTML = ""; // drop old contents
    for (let key of Object.keys( Book.instances)) {
      const book = Book.instances[key];
      const row = tableBodyEl.insertRow(-1);
      row.insertCell(-1).textContent = book.isbn;
      row.insertCell(-1).textContent = book.title;
      row.insertCell(-1).textContent = book.year;
      // if the book has a publisher, show its name
      row.insertCell(-1).textContent =
        book.publisher ? book.publisher.name : "";
    }
    document.getElementById("Book-M").style.display = "none";
    document.getElementById("Book-R").style.display = "block";
  }
};
```

For a multi-valued reference property, the table cell would have to be filled with a list of all associated objects referenced by the property.

2.6.3 Selecting Associated Objects in the *Create* and *Update* Use Cases

For allowing to select objects to be associated with the currently edited object from in the *Create* and *Update* use cases, an HTML selection list (i.e., a select element) is populated with option elements formed from the instances of the associated object type with the help of a utility method fillSelectWithOptions. The HTML select element is defined in the books.html view file:

```
<section id="Book-C" class="UI-Page">
  <h1>Public Library: Create a new book record</h1>
  <form>
    . . .
    <div class="select-one">
      <label>Publisher: <select name="selectPublisher"></select></label>
    </div>
    . . .
  </form>
</section>
```

The *Create* user interface is set up by the following procedure:

```
pl.v.books.create = {
  setupUserInterface: function () {
    const formEl = document.querySelector ("section#Book-C > form"),
        selectPublisherEl = formEl.selectPublisher,
        saveButton = formEl.commit;
    // add event listeners for responsive validation
    formEl.isbn.addEventListener ("input", function () {
     formEl.isbn.setCustomValidity(
        Book.checkIsbnAsId ( formEl.isbn.value).message);
    });
    // set up a single selection list for selecting a publisher
    util.fillSelectWithOptions ( selectPublisherEl,
        Publisher.instances, "name");
    // define event handler for submitButton click events
    saveButton.addEventListener ("click",
        this.handleSaveButtonClickEvent);
    // define event handler for neutralizing the submit event
    formEl.addEventListener ("submit", function (e) {
        e.preventDefault ( );
        formEl.reset ();
    });
    // replace the manage form with the create form
    document.getElementById ("Book-M").style.display = "none";
    document.getElementById ("Book-C").style.display = "block";
    formEl.reset();
  },
  handleSaveButtonClickEvent: function () {
    . . .
  }
};
```

When the user clicks (or touches) the save button, all form control values, including the value of the `select` control, are copied to a `slots` list, which is used as the argument for invoking the `add` method after all form fields have been checked for validity, as shown in the following program listing:

```
handleSaveButtonClickEvent: function () {
    const formEl = document.querySelector("section#Book-C > form");
    const slots = {
        isbn: formEl.isbn.value,
```

```
      title: formEl.title.value,
      year: formEl.year.value,
      publisher_id: formEl.selectPublisher.value
   };
   // validate all form controls and show error messages
   formEl.isbn.setCustomValidity(
   Book.checkIsbnAsId( slots.isbn).message);
   /* . . . (do the same with title and year) */
   // save the input data only if all form fields are valid
   if (formEl.checkValidity()) {
      Book.add ( slots);
   }
}
```

The setupUserInterface code for the *update book* use case is similar.

2.7 Quiz Questions

2.7.1 Question 1: JS Class Model

Which is the correct JS class model for the Committee class derived from the given OO class model?

Committee
name : String {id}
chair : ClubMember

ClubMember
memberId : Integer {id}
firstName : String

Select one:

1. O

Committee
«get/set» name : string {id}
«get/set» chair : ClubMember
checkName(in n : string) : ConstraintViolation
checkChair(in c : ClubMember) : ConstraintViolation
toString() : string
toRecord() : Object

2. O

Committee
«get/set» name : string {id} «get/set» chair : ClubMember
checkName(in n : string) : ConstraintViolation checkNameAsId(in n : string) : ConstraintViolation checkNameAsIdRef(in n : string) : ConstraintViolation checkChair(in c : ClubMember) : ConstraintViolation toString() : string toRecord() : Object

3. O

Committee
«get/set» name : string {id} «get/set» chair : ClubMember
checkName(in n : string) : ConstraintViolation checkNameAsId(in n : string) : ConstraintViolation checkChair(in c : ClubMember) : ConstraintViolation toString() : string toRecord() : Object

3 Implementing Unidirectional Non-Functional Associations with Plain JS

A unidirectional non-functional association is either *one-to-many* or *many-to-many*. In both cases such an association is represented, or implemented, with the help of a *multi-valued* reference property.

In this chapter, we show

1. how to derive a JS class model from an OO class model with *multi-valued reference properties* representing *unidirectional non-functional associations*,
2. how to code the JS class model in the form of JavaScript model classes,
3. how to write the view and controller code based on the model code.

3.1 Implementing Multi-Valued Reference Properties

A multi-valued reference property, such as the property Book::authors, allows storing a collection of references to objects of some type, such as Author objects. When creating a new object of type Book, the constructor function needs to have a parameter for providing a suitable value for this property. We can allow this value to be either a collection of internal object references or of ID references, as shown in the following example:

```
class Book {
  constructor ({isbn, title, year, authors, authorIdRefs,
      publisher, publisher_id}) {
    this.isbn = isbn;
    this.title = title;
    this.year = year;
    // assign object reference or ID reference
    this.authors = authors || authorIdRefs;
    if (publisher || publisher_id) this.publisher = publisher || publisher_id;
  }
  . . .
}
```

Notice that the constructor's parameter record is expected to contain either an authors or an authorIdRefs slot. The JavaScript expression authors || authorIdRefs, using the disjunction operator ||, evaluates to a map authors, if there is a slot with name authors, or to an array authorIdRefs, otherwise. We handle the resulting

https://doi.org/10.1515/9783110500325-004

ambiguity in the property setter by checking the type of the argument as shown in the following code fragment:

```
set authors ( a) {
  this._authors = {};
  if (Array.isArray(a)) { // array of IdRefs
    for (let idRef of a) {
      this.addAuthor( idRef);
    }
  } else { // map of IdRefs to object references
    for (let idRef of Object.keys( a)) {
      this.addAuthor( a[idRef]);
    }
  }
}
```

In JS, a collection-valued reference property can be implemented in two ways:
1. having an array list (a JS array) of object references as its value,
2. having a map as its value, such that the values of the object's standard ID attribute are the keys, which are mapped to internal JS object references.

We prefer using maps for implementing *set-valued* reference properties since they guarantee that each element is unique, while with an array we would have to prevent duplicate elements. Also, an element of a map can be easily deleted (with the help of the delete operator), while this requires more effort in the case of an array. However, for implementing *ordered* (or *nonunique*) association ends corresponding to *ordered-collection*-valued (or bag/sequence-valued) reference properties, we use JS arrays.

3.2 Make a JS Class Model

Our starting point for making a JS class model is the following OO class model:

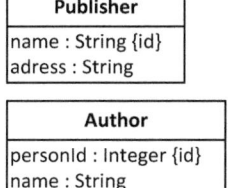

This model contains, in addition to the single-valued reference property Book::publisher representing the unidirectional many-to-one association *Book-**has**-Publisher*, the multi-valued reference property Book::authors representing the unidirectional many-to-many association *Book-**has**-Author*.

For deriving a JS class model from the OO class model we have to follow the same steps as in Section 2.3 and, in addition, we have to take care of multi-valued reference properties, such as Book::authors, for which we

1. create a class-level ***check*** operation, such as checkAuthor, which is responsible for checking the corresponding *referential integrity constraint* for the references to be added to the property's collection;
2. create an **add** operation, such as addAuthor, for adding a reference to the collection;
3. create a **remove** operation, such as removeAuthor, for removing a reference from the collection.

This leads to the following JS class model:

Book
«get/set» isbn[1] : string {id}
«get/set» title[1] : string
«get/set» year[1] : number(int)
«get/set» publisher[0..1] : Publisher
«get/set» authors[1..*] : Author
checkIsbn(in isbn : String) : ConstraintViolation
checkIsbnAsId(in isbn : String) : ConstraintViolation
checkIsbnAsIdRef(in isbn : String) : ConstraintViolation
checkTitle(in title : String) : ConstraintViolation
checkYear(in year : Integer) : ConstraintViolation
checkPublisher(in publisher) : ConstraintViolation
checkAuthor(in author : Author) : ConstraintViolation
addAuthor(in author : Author)
removeAuthor(in author : Author)
toString() : string
toRecord() : Object

Publisher
«get/set» name : string {id}
«get/set» adress : string
checkName(in n : string) : ConstraintViolation
checkNameAsId(in n : string) : ConstraintViolation
checkNameAsIdRef(in n : string) : ConstraintViolation
checkAddress(in a : string) : ConstraintViolation
toString() : string
toRecord() : Object

Author
«get/set» authorId : number(int) {id}
«get/set» name : string
checkAuthorId(in aId : number(int)) : ConstraintViolation
checkAuthorIdAsId(in aId : number(int)) : ConstraintViolation
checkAuthorIdAsIdRef(in aId : number(int)) : ConstraintViolation
checkName(in n : string) : ConstraintViolation
toString() : string
toRecord() : Object

3.3 New Issues

Compared to dealing with a functional association, as discussed in the previous chapter, we now have to deal with the following new technical issues:

1. In the *model* code we now have to take care of ***multi-valued reference properties*** that require implementing

1. an ***add*** and a ***remove*** method, such as addAuthor and removeAuthor, as well as a ***setter*** method for assigning a set of object references with the help of the add method, possibly converting ID references to object references; all three methods may need to check *cardinality constraints*, if there are any;

2. a class-level ***check*** operation, such as checkAuthor, which has to invoke the corresponding check . . . AsIdRef method of the property's range class for checking the property's implicit *referential integrity constraint*;

3. converting a collection of object references to a collection of ID references in the object-to-storage conversion function toRecord.

2. In the *user interface ("view")* code we now have to take care of

1. showing information about a set of associated objects in the property's column of the table view of the *Retrieve/list all* use case; the simplest approach is showing a comma-separated list of ID references, possibly combined with corresponding names; alternatively, HTML lists can be rendered in the property's table data cells;

2. allowing to select a set of associated objects from a list of all existing instances of the property's range class in the *Create* and *Update* use cases.

The last issue, allowing to select a set of associated objects from a list of all instances of some class, can, in general, not be solved with the help of an HTML multiple-select form control because of its poor usability. Whenever the set of selectable options is greater than a certain threshold (defined by the number of options that can be seen on the screen without scrolling), the multiple-select element is no longer usable, and an alternative ***multiple-choice widget*** has to be used.

3.4 Code the Model

Notice that, for simplicity, we do not include the code for all constraint validation checks shown in the JS class model in the code of the example app.

3.4.1 Summary

Code each class of the JS class model as an ES2015 class with implicit getters and setters:

1. Code the property checks in the form of class-level ('static') methods. Take care that all constraints of a property as specified in the JS class model are properly coded in the property checks.

2. For each single-valued property, code the specified getter and setter such that in each setter, the corresponding property check is invoked and the property is only set/unset, if the check does not detect any constraint violation.

3. **For each multi-valued property, code its add and remove operations, as well as the specified get/set operations:**
   1. **Code the add/remove operations as (instance-level) methods that invoke the corresponding property checks.**
   2. **Code the setter such that it invokes the add operation for each item of the collection to be assigned.**
4. Write the code of the serialization function toString() and the object-to-storage conversion function toRecord().
5. Take care of deletion dependencies in the destroy method.

These steps are discussed in more detail in the following sections.

3.4.2 Code the Add and Remove Operations

For the multi-valued reference property Book::authors, we need to code the operations addAuthor and removeAuthor. Both operations accept one parameter denoting an author either by ID reference (the author ID as integer or string) or by an object reference. The code of addAuthor is as follows:

```
addAuthor ( a) {
  // a can be an ID reference or an object reference
  const author_id = (typeof a !== "object") ? parseInt( a) : a.authorId;
  const validationResult = Book.checkAuthor ( author_id);
  if (author_id && validationResult instanceof NoConstraintViolation) {
    // add the new author reference
    let key = String( author_id);
    this._authors[key] = Author.instances[key];
  } else {
    throw validationResult;
  }
}
```

In the removeAuthor method, the author reference is first checked and, if no constraint violation is detected, the corresponding entry in the map this._authors is deleted:

```
removeAuthor ( a) {
  // a can be an ID reference or an object reference
  const author_id = (typeof a !== "object") ?
      parseInt( a) : a.authorId;
  const validationResult = Book.checkAuthor ( author_id);
  if (validationResult instanceof NoConstraintViolation) {
    // delete the author reference
```

```
    delete this._authors [author_id];
  } else {
    throw validationResult;
  }
}
```

For assigning an array of ID references, or a map of object references, to the property Book::authors, the method setAuthors adds them one by one with the help of addAuthor:

```
set authors ( a) {
  this._authors = {};
  if (Array.isArray(a)) { // array of IdRefs
    for (let idRef of a) {
      this.addAuthor( idRef);
    }
  } else { // map of IdRefs to object references
    for (let idRef of Object.keys( a)) {
      this.addAuthor( a[idRef]);
    }
  }
}
```

3.4.3 Choose and Implement a Deletion Policy

For the reference property Book::authors, we have to choose and implement a deletion policy in the destroy method of the Author class. We have to choose between

1. deleting all books (co-)authored by the deleted author (reflecting the logic of *Existential Dependency*);
2. dropping from all books (co-)authored by the deleted author the reference to the deleted author (reflecting the logic of *Existential Independence*).

For simplicity, we go for the second option. This is shown in the following code of the static Author.destroy method where for all concerned book objects the author reference book.authors[authorKey] is dropped:

```
Author.destroy = function (authorId) {
  const author = Author.instances [authorId];
  // delete all dependent book records
  for (let isbn of Object.keys( Book.instances)) {
    let book = Book.instances [isbn];
    if (book.authors[authorId]) delete book.authors[authorId];
```

```
  }
  // delete the author object
  delete Author.instances [authorId];
  console.log("Author " + author.name + " deleted.");
};
```

3.4.4 Serialization and Object-to-Storage Mapping

We need a serialization function toString() for converting an object to a human-readable string representation that can be used for showing an object in a user interface, and an object-to-record mapping function toRecord() converting a typed object to a corresponding record that can be saved in a persistent data-store. In both cases, internal object references are converted to ID references.

The Book::toString() function creates a string representation that may only contain the relevant properties. The simplest method for showing a set of associated objects, like the authors of a book, is creating a comma-separated list of IDs:

```
toString() {
  var bookStr = `Book{ ISBN: ${this.isbn}, title: ${this.title},` +
      `year: ${this.year}`;
  if (this.publisher) bookStr += `, publisher: ${this.publisher.name}`;
  return bookStr +", authors:" +
    Object.keys( this.authors).join(",") +"}";
}
```

The Book::toRecord() function needs to serialize all property slots of an object. This includes deleting the underscore prefix for obtaining the corresponding record field name:

```
toRecord () {
 var rec = {};
 for (let p of Object.keys( this)) {
   // copy only property slots with underscore prefix
   if (p.charAt(0) !== "_") continue;
   switch (p) {
   case "_publisher":
     // convert object reference to ID reference
     if (this._publisher) rec.publisher_id = this._publisher.name;
     break;
   case "_authors":
     // convert map of object references to list of ID references
```

```
  rec.authorIdRefs = [];
 Object.keys( this.authors).forEach( authorIdStr => {
  rec.authorIdRefs.push( parseInt( authorIdStr));
 });
 break;
default:
 // remove underscore prefix
 rec[p.substr(1)] = this[p];
 }
 }
 return rec;
}
```

3.5 Code the View

3.5.1 Showing Information About Associated Objects in *Retrieve/List All*

For showing information about the authors of a book in the *Retrieve/List All* use case, the corresponding cell in the HTML table is filled with a list of the names of all authors with the help of the utility function util.createListFromMap:

```
pl.v.books.retrieveAndListAll = {
 setupUserInterface: function () {
  const tableBodyEl = document.querySelector(
         "section#Book-R>table>tbody");
  tableBodyEl.innerHTML = ""; // drop old contents
  for (let key of Object.keys( Book.instances)) {
   const book = Book.instances[key];
   // create list of authors for this book
   const listEl = util.createListFromMap ( book.authors, "name");
   const row = tableBodyEl.insertRow(-1);
   row.insertCell (-1).textContent = book.isbn;
   row.insertCell (-1).textContent = book.title;
   row.insertCell (-1).textContent = book.year;
   row.insertCell (-1).appendChild( listEl);
   // if the book has a publisher, show its name
   row.insertCell (-1).textContent =
     book.publisher ? book.publisher.name : "";
  }
  document.getElementById("Book-M").style.display = "none";
```

```
    document.getElementById("Book-R").style.display = "block";
  }
};
```

The utility function util.createListFromMap has the following code:

```
createListFromMap: function (m, displayProp) {
  var listEl = document.createElement("ul");
  util.fillListFromMap( listEl, m, displayProp);
  return listEl;
},
fillListFromMap: function (listEl, m, displayProp) {
  const keys = Object.keys ( m);
  // delete old contents
  listEl.innerHTML = "";
  // create list items from object property values
  for (let key of keys) {
    let listItemEl = document.createElement("li");
    listItemEl.textContent = m[key][displayProp];
    listEl.appendChild( listItemEl);
  }
}
```

3.5.2 Selecting Associated Objects in the *Create* Use Case

For allowing to select multiple authors to be associated with the currently edited book in the *Create* use case, a multiple selection list (a select element with multiple="multiple"), as shown in the HTML code below, is populated with the instances of the associated object type.

```
<section id="Book-C" class="UI-Page">
<h1>Public Library: Create a new book record</h1>
<form>
 . . .
 <div class="select-one">
  <label>Publisher: <select name="selectPublisher"></select></label>
 </div>
 <div class="select-many">
  <label>Authors:
   <select name="selectAuthors" multiple="multiple"></select>
  </label>
```

```
  </div>
  . . .
  </form>
</section>
```

The *Create* UI is set up by populating selection lists for selecting the authors and the publisher with the help of a utility method `fillSelectWithOptions` as shown in the following program listing:

```
pl.v.books.create = {
 setupUserInterface: function () {
  const formEl = document.querySelector("section#Book-C > form"),
    selectAuthorsEl = formEl.selectAuthors,
    selectPublisherEl = formEl.selectPublisher,
    saveButton = formEl.commit;
  // add event listeners for responsive validation
   . . .
  // set up a multiple selection list for selecting authors
  util.fillSelectWithOptions( selectAuthorsEl, Author.instances,
    "authorId", {displayProp:"name"});
  // set up a single selection list for selecting a publisher
  util.fillSelectWithOptions( selectPublisherEl,
    Publisher.instances, "name");
  . . .
 },
 handleSaveButtonClickEvent: function () {. . .}
};
```

When the user clicks the save button, all form control values, including the value of any single-select control, are copied to a corresponding field of the `slots` record, which is used as the argument for invoking the `add` method after all form fields have been checked for validity. Before invoking `add`, we first have to create (in the `authorIdRefs` slot) a list of author ID references from the selected options of the multiple authors selection list, as shown in the following program listing:

```
handleSaveButtonClickEvent: function () {
 const formEl = document.querySelector("section#Book-C > form"),
   selAuthOptions = formEl.selectAuthors.selectedOptions;
 const slots = {
   isbn: formEl.isbn.value,
   title: formEl.title.value,
   year: formEl.year.value,
```

```
  authorIdRefs: [],
  publisher_id: formEl.selectPublisher.value
};
 // validate all form controls and show error messages
 . . .
 // check the mandatory value constraint for authors
 formEl.selectAuthors.setCustomValidity(
  (selAuthOptions.length > 0) ? "" : "No author selected!"
 );
 // save the input data only if all form fields are valid
 if (formEl.checkValidity()) {
  // construct a list of author ID references
  for (let opt of selAuthOptions) {
   slots.authorIdRefs.push( opt.value);
  }
  Book.add( slots);
 }
}
```

The *Update* use case is discussed in the next section.

3.5.3 Selecting Associated Objects In the *Update* Use Case

Unfortunately, the multiple-select control is not really usable for displaying and allowing to maintain the set of associated authors in realistic use cases where we have several hundreds or thousands of authors, because the way it renders the choice is visually too scattered. So we have to use a special ***multiple-choice widget*** that allows to add (and remove) objects to (and from) a list of associated objects, as discussed in Section 1.8. In order to show how this widget can replace the multiple-selection list discussed in the previous section, we use it now in the *Update* use case.

For allowing to maintain the set of authors associated with the currently edited book in the *Update* use case, a *multiple-choice widget* as shown in the HTML code below, is populated with the instances of the Author class.

```
<section id="Book-U" class="UI-Page">
 <h1>Public Library: Update a book record</h1>
 <form>
  . . .
  <div class="select-one">
   <label>Publisher: <select name="selectPublisher"></select></label>
  </div>
```

```
  <div class="widget">
    <label for="updBookSelectAuthors">Authors: </label>
    <div class="MultiSelectionWidget" id="updBookSelectAuthors"></div>
  </div>
  . . .
  </form>
</section>
```

The *Update* user interface is set up (in the setupUserInterface procedure shown below) by populating the selection list for selecting the book to be updated with the help of the utility method fillSelectWithOptions. The selection list for assigning a publisher and the multiple-choice widget for assigning the authors of a book are only populated (in handleSubmitButtonClickEvent) when a book to be updated has been chosen.

```
pl.v.books.update = {
 setupUserInterface: function () {
  const formEl = document.querySelector("section#Book-U > form"),
    selectBookEl = formEl.selectBook,
    saveButton = formEl.commit;
// set up the book selection list
  util.fillSelectWithOptions( selectBookEl, Book.instances,
    "isbn", {displayProp:"title"});
  selectBookEl.addEventListener("change", this.
handleBookSelectChangeEvent);
// add event listeners for responsive validation
  . . .
// define event handler for submit button click events
  saveButton.addEventListener("click", this.handleSaveButtonClickEvent);
// handle neutralizing the submit event and resetting the form
  formEl.addEventListener ( 'submit', function (e) {
   var authorsSelWidget = document.querySelector (
       "section#Book-U > form .MultiSelectionWidget");
   e.preventDefault();
   authorsSelWidget.innerHTML = "";
   formEl.reset();
  });
  document.getElementById ("Book-M").style.display = "none";
  document.getElementById ("Book-U").style.display = "block";
  formEl.reset();
 },
```

When a book to be updated has been chosen, the form input fields isbn, title and year, and the select control for updating the publisher, are assigned corresponding values from the chosen book, and the associated authors selection widget is set up:

```
handleBookSelectChangeEvent: function () {
 const formEl = document.querySelector("section#Book-U > form"),
   saveButton = formEl.commit,
   selectAuthorsWidget = formEl.querySelector(".MultiChoiceWidget"),
   selectPublisherEl = formEl.selectPublisher,
   isbn = formEl.selectBook.value;
 if (isbn !== "") {
  let book = Book.instances[isbn];
  formEl.isbn.value = book.isbn;
  formEl.title.value = book.title;
  formEl.year.value = book.year;
  // set up the associated authors selection widget
  util.createMultipleChoiceWidget( selectAuthorsWidget, book.authors,
    Author.instances, "authorId", "name", 1); // minCard=1
  // set up the associated publisher selection list
  util.fillSelectWithOptions( selectPublisherEl, Publisher.instances,
"name");
  // assign associated publisher as the selected option to select element
  if (book.publisher) formEl.selectPublisher.value = book.publisher.name;
  saveButton.disabled = false;
 } else {
  formEl.reset();
  formEl.selectPublisher.selectedIndex = 0;
  selectAuthorsWidget.innerHTML = "";
  saveButton.disabled = true;
 }
},
```

When the user, after updating some values, finally clicks the save button, all form control values, including the value of the single-select control for assigning a publisher, are copied to corresponding slots in a slots record variable, which is used as the argument for invoking the update method after all values have been checked for validity. Before invoking update, a list of ID references to authors to be added, and another list of ID references to authors to be removed, is created (in the authorIdRefsToAdd and authorIdRefsToRemove slots) from the updates that have been recorded in the associated authors selection widget with the help of classList values, as shown in the following program listing:

```
handleSaveButtonClickEvent: function () {
 const formEl = document.querySelector("section#Book-U > form"),
   selectBookEl = formEl.selectBook,
   selectAuthorsWidget = formEl.querySelector(".MultiChoiceWidget"),
   multiChoiceListEl = selectAuthorsWidget.firstElementChild;
 const slots = { isbn: formEl.isbn.value,
    title: formEl.title.value,
year: formEl.year.value,
    publisher_id: formEl.selectPublisher.value
   };
// add event listeners for responsive validation
 . . .
// commit the update only if all form field values are valid
 if (formEl.checkValidity()) {
  // construct authorIdRefs-ToAdd/ToRemove lists from the association list
  let authorIdRefsToAdd=[], authorIdRefsToRemove=[];
  for (let mcListItemEl of multiChoiceListEl.children) {
   if (mcListItemEl.classList.contains("removed")) {
    authorIdRefsToRemove.push( mcListItemEl.getAttribute("data-value"));
   }
   if (mcListItemEl.classList.contains("added")) {
    authorIdRefsToAdd.push( mcListItemEl.getAttribute("data-value"));
   }
  }
  // if the add/remove list is non-empty create a corresponding slot
  if (authorIdRefsToRemove.length > 0) {
   slots.authorIdRefsToRemove = authorIdRefsToRemove;
  }
  if (authorIdRefsToAdd.length > 0) {
   slots.authorIdRefsToAdd = authorIdRefsToAdd;
  }
  Book.update( slots);
  // update the book selection list's option element
  selectBookEl.options[selectBookEl.selectedIndex].text = slots.title;
 }
}
```

3.6 How to Run the App and Get the Code

You can run the example app from our server and download it as a ZIP archive file.

3.7 Points of Attention

We have still included the repetitive code structures (called ***boilerplate code***) in the model layer per class and per property for constraint validation (checks and setters) and per class for the data storage management methods add, update, and destroy. While it is good to write this code a few times for learning app development, you don't want to write it again and again when you work on real projects. For avoiding repetitive boilerplate code, generic forms of these methods are needed, such that they can be reused in all model classes of an app. For instance, the cLASSjs library provides such an approach.

4 Implementing Unidirectional Functional Associations with Java EE

A unidirectional *functional* association is either one-to-one or many-to-one. In both cases such an association is represented, or implemented, with the help of a *single-valued* reference property.

In this chapter, we show

1. how to derive a *data model* in the form of a **Java Entity class model** from an OO class model with single-valued reference properties representing *unidirectional functional associations*,
2. how to code the Java Entity class model in the form of entity classes (implementing *model classes*),
3. how to write the view and controller code based on the entity classes.

4.1 Implementing Single-Valued Reference Properties in Java

A single-valued reference property, such as the property publisher of the object type Book, allows storing internal references to objects of another type, such as Publisher. When creating a new object, the constructor function needs to have a parameter for allowing to assign a suitable value to the reference property. In a typed programming language, such as Java, we may have to take a decision if this value is expected to be an internal object reference or an ID reference. Using the JPA object-to-storage mapping technology, we can work with object references and leave the mapping to corresponding ID references to JPA. The Book class is extended as follows:

```
@Entity @Table( name="books")
@ViewScoped @ManagedBean( name="book")
public class Book {
    . . .
    private Publisher publisher;

    public Book() {}
    public Book( String isbn, String title, Integer year,
        Publisher publisher) {. . .}

    public Publisher getPublisher() {. . .}
```

https://doi.org/10.1515/9783110500325-005

```
    public void setPublisher( Publisher publisher) {. . .}
  . . .
}
```

4.2 Make a Java Entity Class Model

The starting point for making a Java Entity class model is an OO class model like the one shown in Figure 1.10.

As explained before, we obtain the Java Entity class Publisher from the corresponding OO design class by (1) making all properties private, (2) using Java data-type classes (String, Integer, etc.), (3) adding the stereotype «get/set» to properties (specifying public getters and setters), (4) adding a toString function, (5) adding the (class-level) data storage methods create, retrieve, update and delete:

«Java Entity»
Publisher
«get/set» -name : String {id} «get/set» -adress : String
+checkNameAsId(in n : String, in em : EntityManager) : ConstraintViolation +toString() : String +retrieveAll(in em : EntityManager) : List<Publisher> +retrieve(in em : EntityManager, in name : String) : Publisher +create(in em : EntityManager, in name : String, in address : String) +update(in em : EntityManager, in name : String, in address : String) +delete(in em : EntityManager, in name : String)

In a Java Entity class model, for any association end dot in the OO class model, we show the reference property representing the association end and annotate it with the functionality type of the unidirectional association represented by it. In our example, we add a reference property publisher in the entity class Book and annotate it with the association's functionality type manyToOne:

«Java Entity»
Book
«get/set» -isbn[1] : String {id} «get/set» -title[1] : String «get/set» -year[1] : Integer «get/set» -publisher[0..1] : Publisher {manyToOne}
+checkIsbnAsId(in isbn : String, in em : EntityManager) : ConstraintViolation +toString() : string +...()

4.3 New Issues

Compared to the single-class apps discussed in previous, we have to deal with a number of new technical issues:

1. In the *model* code we now have to take care of ***reference properties*** that require
   1. defining ***referential integrity constraints*** with the help of suitable JPA annotations;
   2. extending the code of the `create`, `update` and `delete` methods by taking the reference properties into consideration;
   3. a method for converting between (internal) object references and corresponding (external) ID references in serialization and de-serialization operations.
2. In the *user interface* (view) code we now have to take care of
   1. showing information about associated objects in the *retrieve/list all* use case;
   2. allowing to select an associated object from a list of all existing instances of the target class in the *create object* and *update object* use cases.

4.4 Write the Model Code

The Java Entity class model can be directly coded for getting the model layer code of our Java back-end app.

4.4.1 Summary

1. Code each class from the Java Entity class model as a corresponding entity class.
2. Code an {id} property modifier with the JPA annotation `@Id`
3. Code any property modifier denoting the functionality type of a reference property, such as {manyToOne}, with the corresponding JPA annotation, such as `@ManyToOne`.
4. Code the integrity constraints specified in the model with the help of Java Bean Validation annotations (or custom validation annotations).
5. Code the getters and setters.
6. Code the `create`, `retrieve`, `update` and `delete` storage management operations as class-level methods.

These steps are discussed in more detail in the following sections.

4.4.2 Code Each Class of the Entity Class Model

Each class C of the Java Entity class model is coded as an annotated bean class with name C having a default constructor (with no parameters) and a constructor with entity creation parameters.

For instance, the Book class from the Entity class model is coded in the following way:

```
@Entity @Table( name="books")
@ViewScoped @ManagedBean( name="book")
public class Book {
    @Id @NotNull( message="An ISBN is required!")
    private String isbn;
    @Column( nullable=false)
    @NotNull( message="A title is required!")
    private String title;
    @Column( nullable=false)
    @NotNull( message="A year is required!")
    private Integer year;
    @ManyToOne( fetch=FetchType.EAGER)
    private Publisher publisher;

    public Book() {}
    public Book( String isbn, String title,
            Integer year, Publisher publisher) {
      this.setIsbn( isbn);
      this.setTitle( title);
      this.setYear( year);
      this.setPublisher( publisher);
    }
    . . . // getters, setters, etc.
}
```

The @ManyToOne annotation on the property publisher is used for specifying the functionality type of the association *Book has Publisher* represented by the reference property publisher since it holds that *a book has one publisher* and *a publisher has many books*. This annotation also allows to specify a *fetch type* with the parameter fetch taking one of the following two possible values:

– FetchType.EAGER, implying that a retrieval of an entity includes a retrieval of the associated entity referenced by the entity with this property. In our example, this means that when a Book entity is retrieved, the Publisher entity referenced by the book's publisher property is also retrieved. This behavior is very

useful and it should be used whenever the data to be retrieved can be handled in main memory.
- FetchType.LAZY, implying that referenced entities are not automatically retrieved when a referencing entity is retrieved. In our example, this means that the referenced Publisher entity is not retrieved together with a referencing Book entity, leaving the value of the publisher property set to null. With this fetching behavior, a referenced entity has to be retrieved separately by invoking the reference property's getter in the context of a transaction (in our example by invoking getPublisher).

In the case of a *single-valued* reference property (representing a *functional* association) annotated with either @OneToOne or @ManyToOne, the default value is FetchType.EAGER, so referenced entities are fetched together with referencing entities, while in the case of a *non-functional* association (with either @OneToMany or @ManyToMany), the default value is FetchType.LAZY, so referenced entities are not fetched together with referencing entities, but have to be retrieved separately, if needed.

As a result of these JPA annotations, the following SQL table creation statement for creating the books table is generated:

```
CREATE TABLE IF NOT EXISTS `books` (
    `ISBN` varchar(10) NOT NULL,
    `TITLE` varchar(255) NOT NULL,
    `YEAR` int(11) NOT NULL,
    `PUBLISHER_NAME` varchar(255) DEFAULT NULL
        FOREIGN KEY (`PUBLISHER_NAME`) REFERENCES `publishers` (`NAME`)
);
```

4.4.3 Code the Constraints

Take care that all property constraints specified in the entity class model are properly coded by using suitable Bean Validation annotations. For instance, for the name attribute, we have to use the JPA annotation @Id for specifying that the attribute corresponds to the primary key column of the database table to which the entity class is mapped, and the Bean Validation annotation @NotNull for defining a mandatory value constraint that is checked before an entity is saved to the database.

In the case of the address attribute, we have to define a mandatory value constraint in two forms: with the JPA annotation @Column(nullable=false) for the corresponding table column, and with the Bean Validation annotation @NotNull for the attribute.

```
@Id @NotNull( message="A name is required!")
private String name;

@Column( nullable=false)
@NotNull( message="An address is required!")
 private String address;
```

Notice that, unfortunately, the current Java EE technology requires defining the same constraint twice, once for the database in the form of a JPA annotation, and once for the Java app in the form of a Bean Validation annotation.

4.4.4 Code Getters and Setters

Code the setter operations as (instance-level) methods. The setters only assign values and do not perform any validation, since the property constraints are only checked before save by the Java EE execution environment. The getters simply return the actual values of properties.

4.4.5 Implement a Deletion Policy

For any reference property, we have to choose and implement a deletion policy for taking care of the corresponding object destruction dependency in the delete method of the reference property's range class. In our case, we have to choose between
1. deleting all books published by the deleted publisher;
2. dropping from all books published by the deleted publisher the reference to the deleted publisher.

We choose the second policy, which can only be used inf the case of an optional reference property such as book.publisher. This is shown in the following code of the Publisher.delete method where for all book entities concerned the property book.publisher is cleared:

```
public static void delete( EntityManager em, UserTransaction ut,
     String name) throw Exception {
  ut.begin();
  Publisher publisher = em.find( Publisher.class, name);
  // find all Books which have this publisher
  Query query = em.createQuery(
    "SELECT b FROM Book b WHERE b.publisher.name = :name");
  query.setParameter( "name", name);
```

```
List<Book> books = query.getResultList();
// clear these books' publisher reference
for ( Book b: books) { b.setPublisher( null);}
em.remove( publisher);
ut.commit();
}
```

The method loops through all Book entities referencing the publisher to be destroyed and sets their publisher property to null.

4.4.6 Serialization and De-Serialization

Based on JPA annotations, together with suitable converter classes when needed, serialization (from Java objects to table rows) as well as the corresponding de-serialization (from table columns to Java objects) are performed automatically.

4.5 The View and Controller Layers

The user interface (UI) consists of a start page for navigating to the data management UI pages and one UI page for each object type and data management use case. All these UI pages are defined in the form of JSF view files in subfolders of the WebContent/views/ folder. We create the *Main Menu* page index.xhtml in the subfolder WebContent/views/app with the following content:

```
<!DOCTYPE html>
<html xmlns="http://www.w3.org/1999/xhtml"
    xmlns:ui="..." xmlns:h="..."   xmlns:f="...">
 <ui:composition template="/WEB-INF/templates/page.xhtml">
  <ui:define name="content">
   <h2>Public Library</h2>
   <h:button value="Manage publishers"
     outcome="/views/publishers/index" />
   <h:button value="Manage books" outcome="/views/books/index" />
   <h:form>
    <h:commandButton value="Clear database"
      action="#{appCtrl.clearData()}" />
    <h:commandButton value="Create test data"
      action="#{appCtrl.createTestData()}" />
```

```
    </h:form>
   </ui:define>
  </ui:composition>
</html>
```

It creates the menu buttons which provide the redirects to corresponding views for each of the management pages. Additionally, we need to create a corresponding AppController class which is responsible for the creation and deletion of the test data. The controller is used to combine code of the Publisher.createTestData and Publisher.clearData methods with Book.createTestData and Book.clearData methods as follows:

```
@ManagedBean ( name="appCtrl" )  @SessionScoped
public class AppController {
    @PersistenceContext( unitName="UnidirAssocApp" )
    private EntityManager em;
    @Resource()
    UserTransaction ut;

    public String clearData () {
      try {
        Book.clearData ( em, ut);
        Publisher.clearData ( em, ut);
      } catch ( Exception e) {
        e.printStackTrace ();
      }
      return "index";
    }
    public String createTestData () {
      try {
        Publisher.createTestData ( em, ut);
        Book.createTestData ( em, ut);
      } catch ( Exception e) {
        e.printStackTrace ();
      }
    return "index";
  }
}
```

The deletion of Book and Publisher data must be done in a particular order for avoiding referential integrity violations (books have to be deleted first, before their publishers are deleted).

4.5.1 Initialize the App

Since the code runs in a Tomcat container, the initialization is made internally by the container.

4.5.2 Show Information About Associated Objects in *Retrieve/List All*

In our example we have only one reference property, Book::publisher, which is functional. For showing information about the optional publisher of a book in the *retriev/list all books* use case, the corresponding column in the HTML table is filled with the names of publishers, if there is any:

```
<ui:composition template="/WEB-INF/templates/page.xhtml">
  <ui:define name="content">
    <h:dataTable value="#{bookCtrl.books}" var="b">
      . . .
      <h:column>
        <f:facet name="header">Publisher</f:facet>
        #{b.publisher.name}
      </h:column>
    </h:dataTable>
    <h:button value="Main menu" outcome="index" />
  </ui:define>
</ui:composition>
```

Notice the cascade call used in the #{b.publisher.name} JSF expression, accessing the property name of the publisher which is a property of the book instance b.

4.5.3 Allow Selecting Associated Objects in *Create* and *Update*

In this section, we discuss how to create and update an object which has reference properties, such as a Book object with the reference property publisher.

4.5.3.1 Create the Object-to-String Converter

HTML requires string or number values to populate forms. In our case, the property publisher of the Book class is an object reference. JSF allows converting objects to strings and vice versa by means of *converters*, which are classes annotated with @FacesConverter and implementing the javax.faces.convert.Converter interface:

```
@FacesConverter( value="pl.m.converter.PublisherConverter")
public class PublisherConverter implements Converter {
    @Override
    public Object getAsObject( FacesContext context,
            UIComponent component, String value) {
        PublisherController ac = FacesContext
                .getCurrentInstance()
                .getApplication()
                .evaluateExpressionGet( context, "#{publisherCtrl}",
                    PublisherController.class);
        EntityManager em = ac.getEntityManager();
        if (value == null) return null;
        else return em.find( Publisher.class, value);
    }
    @Override
    public String getAsString( FacesContext context,
            UIComponent component, Object value) {
        if (value == null) return null;
        else if (value instanceof Publisher) {
            return ((Publisher) value).getName ();
        }
        else return null;
    }
}
```

A converter defines two methods: getAsObject and getAsString, which are responsible for the two conversions. For being able to retrieve an object from a database we need an EntityManager, which can be obtained from a controller (e.g., the managed bean publisherCtrl). The controller can be obtained via the FacesContext singleton:

```
PublisherController ac = FacesContext.getCurrentInstance()
    .getApplication()
    .evaluateExpressionGet( context, "#{publisherCtrl}",
        PublisherController.class);
```

In addition, we need to add a `getEntityManager` method in the controller class as follows:

```
@ManagedBean( name="publisherCtrl") @SessionScoped
public class PublisherController {
    @PersistenceContext( unitName="UnidirAssocApp")
    private EntityManager em;
    @Resource()
    UserTransaction ut;

    public EntityManager getEntityManager() {
        return this.em;
    }
    . . .
}
```

JSF needs to compare two publisher instances, when the `publisher` list has to auto-select the current publisher, in the *update book* use case. For this reason, the `Publisher` model class needs to implement the equals method. In our case, two publishers are "one and the same", if the values of their name property are equal:

```
@Override
public boolean equals( Object obj) {
    if (obj instanceof Publisher) {
        Publisher publisher = (Publisher) obj;
        return ( this.name.equals( publisher.name));
    } else return false;
}
```

4.5.3.2 Write the View Code

To allow selection of objects which have to be associated with the currently edited object from a list in the *create* and *update* use cases, an HTML selection list (a select element) is populated with the instances of the associated object type with the help of a `h:selectOneMenu` element. The create.xhtml file in the folder WebContent/views/books/ is updated as follows:

```
<ui:composition template="/WEB-INF/templates/page.xhtml">
 <ui:define name="content">
  <h:form id="createBookForm" styleClass="pure-form pure-form-aligned">
```

```
<h:panelGrid columns="3">
  . . .
  <h:outputLabel for="publisher" value="Publisher:" />
  <h:selectOneMenu id="publisher" value="#{book.publisher}">
    <f:selectItem itemValue="" itemLabel="---" />
    <f:selectItems value="#{publisherCtrl.publishers}" var="p"
                   itemLabel="#{p.name}" itemValue="#{p}" />
    <f:converter converterId="pl.m.converter.PublisherConverter" />
  </h:selectOneMenu>
  <h:message for="publisher" errorClass="error" />
</h:panelGrid>
<h:commandButton value="Create"
    action="#{bookCtrl.create( book.isbn, book.title,
    book.year, book.publisher.name)}" />
</h:form>
</ui:define>
</ui:composition>
```

The converter is specified by using the f:converter element and its associated
@converterId attribute. The value of this attribute must be the same as the one
specified by the value attribute of the annotation @FacesConverter used when the
converter class is defined, e.g.,

```
@FacesConverter( value = "pl.m.converter.PublisherConverter")
```

In general, the converter's local class name can be used (e.g., PublisherConverter),
or the fully qualified class name, if there is a risk of naming conflicts (e.g., pl.m.
converter.PublisherConverter). We recommend using the fully qualified name in
all cases.

The #{publisherCtrl.publishers} expression results in calling the getPublishers
method of the PublisherController class, which is responsible to return the list
of available publishers:

```
public List<Publisher> getPublishers () {
    return Publisher.retrieveAll ( em);
}
```

The creation of the book is obtained by using the h:commandButton element. It results in the invocation of the create method of the BookController class:

```
public String create( String isbn, String title, Integer year,
      Publisher publisher) {
  try {
    Book.create( em, ut, isbn, title, year, publisher);
    // Enforce clearing the form after creating the Book row
    FacesContext facesContext = FacesContext.getCurrentInstance();
    facesContext.getExternalContext().getRequestMap().remove( "book");
  } catch ( EntityExistsException e) {
    try {
      ut.rollback();
    } catch ( Exception e1) {
      e1.printStackTrace();
    }
    e.printStackTrace();
  } catch ( Exception e) {
    e.printStackTrace();
  }
  return "create";
}
```

It simply calls the Book.create method for creating a new row in the books table.

The code for the *update book* use case is very similar, the only important difference is the addition of the select element (i.e., using the h:selectOneMenu JSF element) for allowing to select the book to update:

```
<ui:composition template="/WEB-INF/templates/page.xhtml">
 <ui:define name="content">
 <h:form id="createBookForm" styleClass="pure-form pure-form-aligned">
 <h:panelGrid columns="3">
 . . .
 <h:outputLabel for="selectBook" value="Select book: " />
 <h:selectOneMenu id="selectBook" value="#{book.isbn}">
 <f:selectItem itemValue="" itemLabel="---" />
 <f:selectItems value="#{bookCtrl.books}" var="b"
     itemValue="#{b.isbn}" itemLabel="#{b.title}" />
 <f:ajax listener="#{bookCtrl.refreshObject( book)}"
     render="isbn title year publisher"/>
 </h:selectOneMenu>
 <h:message for="selectedBook"/>
 . . .
```

```
    </h:panelGrid>
    <h:commandButton value="Create" action="#{bookCtrl.create (
      book.isbn, book.title, book.year, book.publisher.name)}" />
   </h:form>
  </ui:define>
 </ui:composition>
```

5 Unidirectional Non-Functional Associations with Java EE

A unidirectional non-functional association is either *one-to-many* or *many-to-many*. In both cases such an association is represented with the help of a *multi-valued* reference property.

In this chapter, we show

1. how to derive a ***Java Entity class model*** from an OO class model with *multi-valued reference properties* representing *unidirectional non-functional associations*,
2. how to code the Java Entity class model in the form of entity classes (implementing *model classes*),
3. how to write the view and controller code based on the model code.

5.1 Implementing Multi-Valued Reference Properties in Java

A multi-valued reference property, such as Book::authors, allows storing a collection of internal references to objects of some type, such as references to Author objects. When creating a new object of type Book, the constructor function needs to have a parameter for providing a suitable value for this property. In general, this value can be a set of internal object references or of ID references. With JPA, we use object references:

```
@Entity @Table ( name="books")
@ManagedBean ( name="book")
@ViewScoped
public class Book {
    . . .
    private Set<Author> authors;

    public Book() { // required by JPA @Entity annotation!}
    public Book( String isbn, String title, Integer year,
            Publisher publisher, Set<Author> authors) {. . .}

    public Set<Author> getAuthors() { return this.authors;}
    public void setAuthors( Set<Author> authors) { this.authors = authors;}
    . . .
}
```

https://doi.org/10.1515/9783110500325-006

5.2 Make a Java Entity Class Model

Our starting point for making a Java Entity class model is the following OO class model:

Book
isbn[1] : String {id}
title[1] : String
year[1] : Integer
publisher[0..1] : Publisher
authors[*] : Author

Publisher
name : String {id}
adress : String

Author
personId : Integer {id}
name : String

This model contains, in addition to the single-valued reference property Book::publisher representing the unidirectional many-to-one association *Book*-**has**-*Publisher*, the multi-valued reference property Book::authors representing the unidirectional many-to-many association *Book*-**has**-*Author*.

Recall that we obtain a Java Entity class, like Author, from the corresponding class in the OO class model, by (1) making all properties private, (2) using Java data-type classes, (3) adding public getters and setters, (4) adding a toString function, (5) adding the data storage methods create, retrieve, update and delete:

«Java Entity» **Author**
«get/set» -personId : Integer {id} «get/set» -name : String
+checkPersonIdAsId(in pId : Integer, in em : EntityManager) : ConstraintViolation +toString() : String +...()

In the Java Entity class model, any reference property specified in the OO class model is annotated with the functionality type of the association represented by it.

In our example, we annotate the reference property authors in the Entity class Book with manyToMany:

«Java Entity» Book
«get/set» -isbn[1] : String {id}
«get/set» -title[1] : String
«get/set» -year[1] : Integer
«get/set» -publisher[0..1] : Publisher {manyToOne}
«get/set» -authors[*] : Author {manyToMany}
+checkIsbnAsId(in isbn : String, in em : EntityManager) : ConstraintViolation
+addAuthor(in author : Author)
+removeAuthor(in author : Author)
+toString() : string
+...()

5.3 New Issues

Compared to dealing with a unidirectional functional association, as discussed in the previous section, we have to deal with the following new technical issues:

1. In *model classes* we now have to take care of **multi-valued reference proper-ties** that have to be annotated with @OneToMany or @ManyToMany.
2. In the *user interface* code we now have to take care of
   1. showing information about a collection of associated objects in the view table columns that render multi-valued reference properties in the *retrieve/ list all objects* use case;
   2. allowing to select a collection of associated objects from a list of all existing instances of the target class in the *create object* and *update object* use cases.

The last issue, allowing to select a collection of associated objects from a list of all existing instances of some class, in general, cannot be solved with the help of an HTML select multiple form element because of usability problems. Whenever the set of selectable options is greater than a certain threshold (defined by the number of options that can be seen on the screen without scrolling), the HTML select multiple element is no longer usable, and an alternative *multi-selection widget* has to be used.

5.4 Write the Model Code

The Java Entity class model can be directly coded for implementing the model layer of our Java back-end app.

5.4.1 Summary

1. Code each class of the Java Entity class model as a corresponding entity class.
2. Code any {id} property modifier with the JPA property annotation @Id.
3. Code any property modifier denoting the functionality type of a reference property, such as {manyToOne}, with the corresponding JPA annotation, such as @ManyToOne.
4. Code the integrity constraints specified in the model with the help of Java Bean Validation annotations (or custom validation annotations).
5. Code the getters and setters as well as the *add* and *remove* methods for multi-valued properties.
6. Code the create, retrieve, update and delete storage management operations as class-level methods.

These steps are discussed in more detail in the following sections.

5.4.2 Code Each Class of the Java Entity Class Model

For the multi-valued reference property Book::authors, we use a parametrized Set type:

```
@Entity @Table ( name="books")
@ViewScoped @ManagedBean ( name="book")
public class Book {
    . . .
    @ManyToMany ( fetch=FetchType.EAGER)
    private Set<Author> authors;

    public Book() {}
    public Book( String isbn, String title, Integer year,
        Publisher publisher, Set<Author> authors) {. . .}
    . . .
    public Set<Author> getAuthors() { return this.authors;}
    public void setAuthors( Set<Author> authors) { this.authors=authors;}
    . . .
}
```

The JPA annotation @ManyToMany allows to specify the **Many-To-Many** relation between the Book and Author. The annotation parameter FetchType.EAGER is used, so when a Book instance is created, the list of authors is populated with the corresponding Author instances. As a result of this annotation, a relation table between Book and Author is created, and the resulting SQL code is shown below:

```
CREATE TABLE IF NOT EXISTS `books_author` (
  `Book_ISBN` varchar(10) NOT NULL,
  `authors_PERSONID` int(11) NOT NULL
);
```

The resulting class name is the underscore-separated concatenation of the corresponding table names (e.g., books_author). The primary key columns from each of the two tables are used to implement the relation. The corresponding column names are created as follows:

- for the table (e.g., books) which correspond to the class with the @ManyToMany annotation (e.g., Book), the class name is used as well as the primary key column name, (e.g., Book_ISBN).
- for the other table (e.g., authors), the table name is concatenated with the primary key column name, (e.g., authors_PERSONID).

It is possible to control these parameters, i.e., table name and relation column names, by using the @JoinTable annotation. To obtain a custom named relation table, e.g., books_authors and the corresponding custom named columns, e.g., book_isbn and author_personid, one can use:

```
@JoinTable( name="books_authors",
    joinColumns = {@JoinColumn( name="book_isbn",
    referencedColumnName="ISBN")},
    inverseJoinColumns = {@JoinColumn( name="author_personid",
                            referencedColumnName="PERSONID")}
```

In our application, we keep the default, so a @JoinTable annotation is not used.

The corresponding Author class is coded as a Java Entity class with suitable annotations:

```
@Entity @Table ( name="author")
@ManagedBean ( name="author") @ViewScoped
public class Author {
    // Properties
    @Id @PositiveInteger
    private Integer personId;
    @Column ( nullable=false)
    @NotNull ( message="A name is required!")
    private String name;
```

```
@Column ( nullable=false)
@NotNull ( message="A date of birth is required!")
@Past private Date dateOfBirth;
@Past private Date dateOfDeath;
// Constructors
. . .
// Setters/getters
. . .
// Data management operations
. . .
}
```

In addition to defining properties, the entity class needs to define constructors, setters/getters and data management operations:

```
@Entity @Table( name="author")
@ManagedBean( name="author") @ViewScoped
public class Author {
    // Properties
    . . .
    // Constructors
    public Author() {}
    public Author( Integer personId, String name,
        Date dateOfBirth, Date dateOfDeath) {. . .}
    // Setters/getters
    . . .
    // Data management operations
    public static void create( EntityManager em, UserTransaction ut,
        Integer personId, String name, Date dateOfBirth,
        Date dateOfDeath) {. . .}
    public static void update(. . .) {. . .}
    public static void delete(. . .) {. . .}
}
```

5.4.3 Implement a Deletion Policy

For the reference property Book::authors, we have to implement a deletion policy in the delete method of the Author class. If we just try to delete an author, and the author is referenced by any of the book records, then an integrity constraint

violation exception is raised, and the author cannot be deleted. We have two possi-
blitities for dealing with this situation:
1. delete all books (co-)authored by the deleted author;
2. drop from all books (co-)authored by the deleted author the reference to the de-
    leted author.

We go for the second option. This is shown in the following code of the Author.de-
lete method:

```
public static void delete( EntityManager em, UserTransaction ut,
      Integer personId) throws Exception {
   ut.begin();
   Author author = em.find( Author.class, personId);
   // Find all books of this author
   Query query = em.createQuery( "SELECT DISTINCT b FROM Book b "+
      "INNER JOIN b.authors a WHERE a.personId = :personId");
   query.setParameter( "personId", personId);
   List<Book> books = query.getResultList();
   // Remove the author reference from the books' authors list
   for (Book b : books) {
       b.getAuthors().remove( author);
 }
   // Delete the author record (table row)
   em.remove( author);
   ut.commit();
 }
```

Essentially, the delete operation consists of three steps:
1. Create a JPQL query which selects all books of this author (since this is a unidi-
    rectional association from books to authors, the books of an author are not di-
    rectly accessible from an author).
2. For every found book referencing this author, we have to remove the author ref-
    erence from its authors list.
3. Finally, delete the author record.

5.4.4 Serialization and De-Serialization

In Java EE, the serialization from objects to corresponding database records as well
as the de-serialization from database records to objects are performed automatically
by the Java EE execution environment based on JPA annotations and converter classes for custom conversions.

5.5 Write the User Interface Code

5.5.1 Show Information About Associated Objects in *Retrieve/List All*

For showing information about the authors of a book in the *retrieve/list all books* use case, the corresponding cell in the HTML table has to be filled with a list of the names of all authors. For this, we implement a method in the Book class which returns the serialized list of author names (in the form, *authorName_1, authorName_2, . . ., authorName_n*):

```java
public String getAuthorNames() {
  String result = "";
  int i = 0, n = 0;
  if ( this.authors != null) {
    n = this.authors.size();
    for ( Author author : this.authors) {
      result += author.getName();
      if ( i< n - 1) {
        result +=", ";
      }
      i++;
    }
  }
  return result;
}
```

In the view file retrieveAndListAll.xhtml in the folder WebContent/views/books/, this method is invoked in the JSF expression of the "Authors" column:

```xml
<ui:composition template="/WEB-INF/templates/page.xhtml">
  <ui:define name="content">
    <h:dataTable value="#{bookController.books}" var="b">
      . . .
      <h:column>
        <f:facet name="header">Publisher</f:facet>
        #{b.publisher.name}
      </h:column>
      <h:column>
        <f:facet name="header">**Authors**</f:facet>
        #{**b.authorNames**}
      </h:column>
    </h:dataTable>
```

```
    <h:button value="Back" outcome="index" />
  </ui:define>
</ui:composition>
```

Recall that using b.authorNames results in invoking a method named getAuthorNames on the given b object.

5.5.2 Allow Selecting Associated Objects in *Create*

For allowing to select multiple authors to be associated with a book in the *create book* use case, a multiple selection list (a select element with multiple="multi-ple"), as shown in the facelet code below, is populated with the instances of the associated object type. The following code is part of the create.xhtml view file in the folder WebContent/views/books/:

```
<ui:composition template="/WEB-INF/templates/page.xhtml">
  <ui:define name="content">
    <h:form id="createBookForm">
      <h:panelGrid columns="3">
        . . .
        <h:outputLabel for="authors" value="Authors:"/>
        <h:selectManyListbox id="authors" value="#{book.authors}">
          <f:selectItems value="#{authorController.authors}" var="a"
              itemLabel="#{a.name}" itemValue="#{a}"/>
          <f:converter converterId="AuthorConverter"/>
        </h:selectManyListbox>
        <h:message for="authors" errorClass="error"/>
      </h:panelGrid>
      <h:commandButton value="Create" action="#{bookController.create(
        book.isbn, book.title, book.year, book.publisher, book.authors)}"/>
    </h:form>
    <h:button value="Back" outcome="index" />
  </ui:define>
</ui:composition>
```

Remember that we have to add the equals method for the Author model class. In our case, two authors are "one and the same" if the values of their personId property are equal:

```
@Override
public boolean equals( Object obj) {
   if (obj instanceof Author) {
      Author author = (Author) obj;
         return (this.personId.equals( author.personId));
   } else return false;
}
```

Like in the case of Publisher, a JSF converter class is used to serialize authors objects to display strings, when the select list is populated, and back to objects, when the create method of the BookController is called (the "Create" button was pushed by the user). The BookController.create method is extended with a new parameter, the authors list:

```
public String create( String isbn, String title, Integer year,
      Publisher publisher, Set<Author> authors) {
   try {
      Book.create ( em, ut, isbn, title, year, publisher, authors);
      // Enforce clearing the form after creating the Book record
      FacesContext facesContext = FacesContext.getCurrentInstance();
      facesContext.getExternalContext().getRequestMap().remove( "book");
   } catch ( EntityExistsException e) {
      try {
      ut.rollback();} catch (Exception e1) {
         e1.printStackTrace();
      }
      e.printStackTrace();
   } catch (Exception e) {
      e.printStackTrace();
   }
   return "create";
}
```

The *update book* use case is similar to the *create book* use case.

5.6 Run the App and Get the Code

For running your application, you may first have to stop your Tomcat/TomEE server (with bin/shutdown.bat for Windows or bin/shutdown.sh for Linux). Next, download and unzip our ZIP archive file containing all the source code of the app and the ANT script file that you have to edit (modify the `server.folder` property value). Now, execute the following command in your console or terminal:

```
ant deploy -Dappname=UnidirectionalAssociationApp
```

Finally, start your Tomcat web server (by using bin/startup.bat for Windows OS or `bin/startup.sh` for Linux). Please be patient, this can take some time depending on the speed of your computer. It will be ready when the console displays the following message: *INFO: Initializing Mojarra [some library versions and paths are shown here] for context '/subtypingapp'*. Finally, open a web browser and type:

```
http://localhost:8080/UnidirectionalAssociationApp/WebContent/views/app/
index.xhtml
```

5.7 Sets Versus Ordered Sets as the Values of Reference Properties

Recall that a *set* is an unordered collection that has unique elements, while a *list* is an ordered collection that may contain the same element more than once.

When a non-functional association end is *ordered*, like `Book::authors`, in the class diagram shown in Figure 5.1, this implies that the range of the corresponding reference property needs to be an ordered collection type, such as the Java collection interface types `SortedSet` and List.

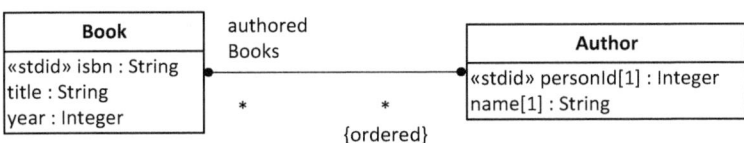

Figure 5.1: A set-valued reference property authoredBooks and an ordered-set-valued reference property authors.

In theory, set-valued reference properties should be defined with Set<T>, such as declaring Set<Book> as the range of `Author::authoredBooks`, while ordered-set-valued reference properties should be defined with SortedSet<T>, such as declaring SortedSet<Author> as the range of `Book::authors`. The Java interface type Set is typically implemented by the Java class HashSet, while SortedSet is typically implemented by TreeSet.

However, if there is no concern about avoiding duplicate elements, both set-valued and ordered-set-valued reference properties can also be defined with the generic interface type List<T> as their range, which is typically implemented with ArrayList.

When the main use cases are adding elements to the collection and later iterate over them, the best choice is using List implemented by ArrayList, which is more memory efficient than LinkedList or any implementation of Set, and has fast insertion, iteration, and random access. Using HashSet provides a performance benefit only in the use case of finding an element in the collection.

6 Unidirectional Associations Practice Projects

All projects include the following tasks:
1. Make an **OO class model** derived from the given design model. Hint: replace associations with corresponding reference properties.
2. Make a **JavaScript class model** or a **Java Entity class model** derived from the OO class model. Hint: add check and setter methods.
3. Code your JS class model or Java Entity class model, following the provided guidelines.

Make sure that your pages comply with the XML syntax of HTML5, and that your JavaScript code complies with our Coding Guidelines and is checked with (JSHint).

6.1 Assign a Director and Actors to a Movie

This project is based on the information design model shown below. The app from the previous assignments is to be extended by adding the possibility to manage data about the actors and the director of a movie. This is achieved by adding a model class Person and two unidirectional associations between Movie and Person:
1. a many-to-one association assigning exactly one person as the **director** of a movie, and
2. a many-to-many association assigning zero or more persons as the **actors** of a movie.

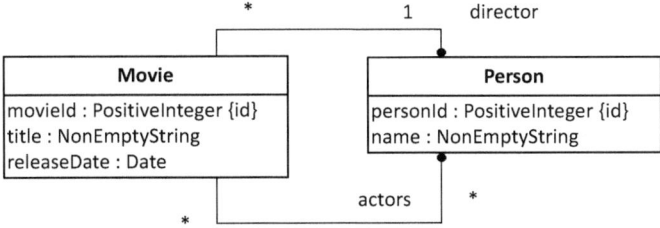

https://doi.org/10.1515/9783110500325-007

You can use the following sample data for testing your app:

Movies

Movie ID	Title	Release date	Director	Actors
1	Pulp Fiction	1994-05-12	3	4, 5
2	Star Wars	1977-05-25	2	6, 7
3	Dangerous Liaisons	1988-12-16	1	8, 4

People

Person ID	Name
1	Stephen Frears
2	George Lucas
3	Quentin Tarantino
4	Uma Thurman
5	John Travolta
6	Ewan McGregor
7	Natalie Portman
8	Keanu Reeves

More movie data can be found on the IMDb website.

6.2 Assign Cities and a Capital to a Country, and Members to an Organization

This project is based on the information design model shown below. The corresponding app from the previous assignments is to be extended by adding the possibility to manage data about *international organizations*, with countries as *members*, and about *cities*, as *capitals* and *headquarter locations*. This is achieved by adding corresponding model classes InternationalOrganization and City, and the following unidirectional associations:

1. a many-to-many association between InternationalOrganization and Country assigning zero or more countries as the **members** of an international organization, and

2. a one-to-one association between `Country` and `City` assigning exactly one city as the ***capital*** of a country,
3. a one-to-many association between `Country` and `City` assigning cities to a country.

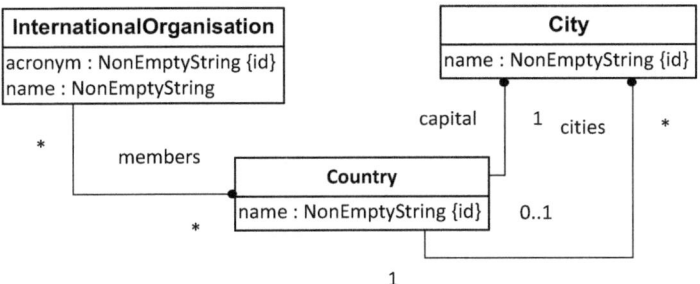

You can use the following sample data for testing your app:

International organizations

Acronym	Name	Members
UN	United Nations	Germany, France, Russia
WHO	World Health Organization	Germany, France, Russia
NATO	North Atlantic Treaty Organization	Germany, France

Countries

Name	Capital	Cities
France	Paris	Marseille, Lyon, Paris
Germany	Berlin	Berlin, Hamburg, Frankfurt
Russia	Moscow	Moscow, Novosibirsk

Cities

Name
Berlin
Frankfurt
Hamburg

(continued)

Cities
Name
Lyon
Marseille
Moscow
Novosibirsk
Paris

More data about countries can be found in the CIA World Factbook.

7 Bidirectional Associations

In OO modeling and programming, a *bidirectional* association is an association that is represented as a pair of mutually inverse reference properties, which allow 'navigation' (object access) in both directions.

The model shown in Figure 7.1 below (about publishers, books and their authors) serves as our running example. Notice that it contains two bidirectional associations, as indicated by the ownership dots at both association ends.

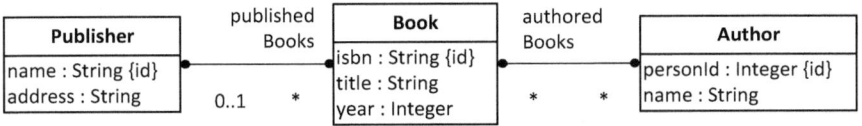

Figure 7.1: The Publisher-Book-Author information design model with two bidirectional associations.

7.1 Inverse Reference Properties

For being able to easily retrieve the committees that are chaired or co-chaired by a club member, we add two reference properties to our *Committee-ClubMember* example model: the property of a club member to be the chair of a committee (ClubMember::chairedCommittee) and the property of a club member to be the co-chair of a committee (ClubMember::coChairedCommittee). We assume that any club member may chair or co-chair at most one committee (where the disjunction is non-exclusive). So, we get the following model:

Committee	ClubMember
name : String chair : ClubMember	chairedCommittee[0..1] : Committee coChairedCommittee[0..1] : Committee

Notice that there is a close correspondence between the two reference properties Committee::chair and ClubMember::chairedCommittee. They are the **inverse** of each other: when the club member Tom is the chair of the budget committee, expressed by the tuple *("budget committee", "Tom")*, then the budget committee is the committee chaired by the club member Tom, expressed by the inverse tuple *("Tom", "budget committee")*. For expressing this inverse correspondence in the diagram, we append an inverse property constraint, inverse of chair, in curly braces

https://doi.org/10.1515/9783110500325-008

to the declaration of the property `ClubMember::chairedCommittee`, and a similar one to the property `Committee::chair`, as shown in the following diagram:

Committee
name : String
chair : ClubMember {inverse of chairedCommittee}

ClubMember
chairedCommittee[0..1] : Committee {inverse of chair}
coChairedCommittee[0..1] : Committee

Using the reference path notation of OOP languages, with *c* referencing a `Committee` object, we obtain the equation:

$$c.\text{chair.chairedCommittee} = c \tag{7.1}$$

Or, the other way around, with *m* referencing a `ClubMember` object, we obtain the equation:

$$m.\text{chairedCommittee.chair} = m \tag{7.2}$$

Notice that when a property p_2 is the inverse of a property p_1, this implies that, the other way around, p_1 is the inverse of p_2. Therefore, when we declare the property `ClubMember::chairedCommittee` to be the inverse of `Committee::chair`, then, implicitly, `Committee::chair` is the inverse of `ClubMember::chairedCommittee`. We therefore call `Committee::chair` and `ClubMember::chairedCommittee` a ***pair of mutually inverse reference properties***. Having such a pair in a model implies ***redundancy*** because each of the two involved reference properties can be derived from the other by inversion. This type of redundancy implies *data storage overhead* and *update overhead*, which is the price to pay for the bidirectional navigability that supports efficient object access in both directions.

For maintaining the duplicate information of a mutually inverse reference property pair, it is common to treat one of the two involved properties as the *master*, and the other one as the *slave*, and take this distinction into consideration in the code of the change methods (such as the property setters) of the affected model classes. We indicate the slave of an inverse reference property pair in a model diagram by declaring the slave property to be a ***derived*** property using the UML notation of a slash (/) as a prefix of the property name as shown in the following diagram:

Committee
name : String
chair : ClubMember

ClubMember
/chairedCommittee[0..1] : Committee {inverse of chair}
coChairedCommittee[0..1] : Committee

The property `chairedCommittee` in `ClubMember` is now *derived* (as indicated by its slash prefix). Its annotation {`inverse of chair`} defines a *derivation rule* according to which it is derived by inverting the property `Committee::chair`.

In a UML class diagram, the derivation of a property can be specified by an OCL *derive* expression that evaluates to the value of the derived property for a given object. In the case of a property being the inverse of another property, specified by the constraint expression {inverse of *anotherProperty*} appended to the property declaration, the derivation expression is implied. In our example, for any club member object m, it evaluates to the committee object c such that c.chair = m. In OCL, this derivation rule would be expressed like so

```
context ClubMember::chairedCommittee: Committee
derive:
  if Committee.allInstances().exists( c | c.chair = self) then c
```

There are two ways how to realize the derivation of a property: it may be *derived on read* via a read-time computation of its value, or it may be *derived on update* via an update-time computation performed whenever one of the variables in the derivation expression (typically, another property) changes its value. The latter case corresponds to a *materialized view* in a database. While a reference property that is derived on read may not guarantee efficient navigation, because the on-read computation may create unacceptable latencies, a reference property that is derived on update does provide efficient navigation.

When we designate an inverse reference property as derived by prefixing its name with a slash (/), we indicate that it is derived on update. For instance, the property /chairedCommittee in the example above is derived on update from the property chair.

In the case of a derived reference property, we have to deal with **life-cycle dependencies** between the affected model classes requiring special change management mechanisms based on the functionality type of the represented association (either *one-to-one, many-to-one* or *many-to-many*).

In our example of the derived inverse reference property ClubMember::chairedCommittee, which is single-valued and optional, this means that

1. whenever a new committee object is created (with a mandatory chair assignment), the corresponding ClubMember::chairedCommittee property has to be assigned accordingly;
2. whenever the chair property is updated (that is, a new chair is assigned to a committee), the corresponding ClubMember::chairedCommittee property has to be unset for the club member who was the previous chair and set for the one being the new chair;
3. whenever a committee object is destroyed, the corresponding ClubMember::chairedCommittee property has to be unset.

In the case of a derived inverse reference property that is multi-valued while its inverse base property is single-valued (like `Publisher::publishedBooks` in Figure 7.4 below being derived from `Book::publisher`), the life cycle dependencies imply that

1. whenever a new 'base object' (such as a book) is created, the corresponding inverse property has to be updated by adding a reference to the new base object to its value set (like adding a reference to the new book object to `Publisher::publishedBooks`);

2. whenever the base property is updated (e.g., a new publisher is assigned to a book), the corresponding inverse property (in our example, `Publisher::publishedBooks`) has to be updated as well by removing the old object reference from its value set and adding the new one;

3. whenever a base object (such as a book) is destroyed, the corresponding inverse property has to be updated by removing the reference to the base object from its value set (like removing a reference to the book object to be destroyed from `Publisher::publishedBooks`).

Notice that from a purely computational point of view, we are free to choose either of the two mutually inverse reference properties (like `Book::authors` and `Author::authoredBooks`) to be the master. However, in many cases, associations represent asymmetrical ontological existence dependencies that dictate which of the two mutually inverse reference properties is the master. For instance, the authorship association between the classes `Book` and `Author` represents an ontological existence dependency of books on their authors. A book existentially depends on its author(s), while an author does not existentially depend on any of her books. Consequently, the corresponding object lifecycle dependency between `Book` and `Author` implies that their bidirectional association is maintained by maintaining `Author` references in `Book::authors` as the natural choice of master property, while `Author::authoredBooks` is the slave property, which is derived from `Book::authors`.

7.2 Making an OO Class Model

Since classical OO programming languages do not support explicit associations as first class citizens, but only classes with reference properties representing implicit associations, we have to eliminate all explicit associations for obtaining an OO class model.

7.2.1 The Basic Procedure

The starting point of our *association elimination* procedure is an information design model with various kinds of unidirectional and bidirectional associations, such as the model shown in Figure 7.1 above. If the model still contains any non-directed associations, we first have to turn them into directed ones by making a decision on the ownership of their ends, which is typically based on navigability requirements.

Notice that both associations in the *Publisher-Book-Author* information design model, *publisher-publishedBooks* and *authoredBooks-authors* (or *Authorship*), are bidirectional as indicated by the ownership dots at both association ends. For eliminating all explicit associations from an information design model, we have to perform the following steps:

1. ***Eliminate unidirectional associations***, connecting a source with a target class, by replacing them with a reference property in the source class such that the target class is its range.
2. ***Eliminate bidirectional associations*** by replacing them with a pair of mutually inverse reference properties.

7.2.2 How to Eliminate Unidirectional Associations

A unidirectional association connecting a source with a target class is replaced with a corresponding reference property in its source class having the target class as its range. Its multiplicity is the same as the multiplicity of the target association end. Its name is the name of the association end, if there is any, otherwise it is set to the name of the target class (possibly pluralized, if the reference property is multi-valued).

7.2.3 How to Eliminate Bidirectional Associations

A bidirectional association, such as the authorship association between the classes Book and Author in the model shown in Figure 7.1 above, is replaced with a pair of mutually inverse reference properties, such as Book::authors and Author:: authoredBooks. Since both reference properties represent the same information (the same set of binary relationships), it's an option to consider one of them being the "master" and the other one the "slave", which is derived from the master. We discuss the two cases of a one-to-one and a many-to-many association

1. In the case of a bidirectional one-to-one association, this leads to a pair of mutually inverse single-valued reference properties, one in each of the two associated classes. Since both of them represent essentially the same information (the same collection of links/relationships), one has to choose which of them is considered the master property, such that the other one is the slave property, which is derived from the master property by inversion. In the class diagram, the slave property is designated as a *derived property* that is automatically updated whenever 1) a new master object is created, 2) the master reference property is updated, or 3) a master object is destroyed. This transformation is illustrated in Figure 7.2.

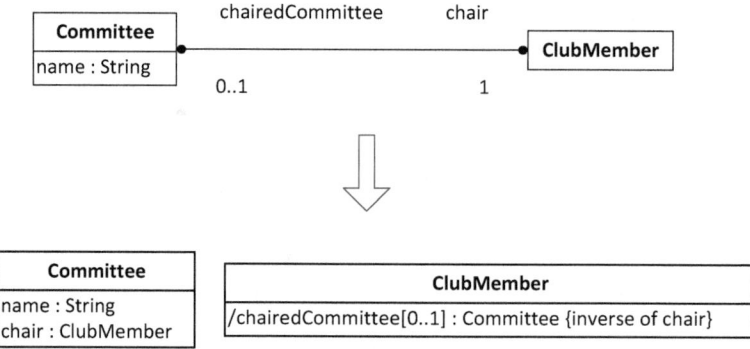

Figure 7.2: Turn a bidirectional one-to-one association into a master-slave pair of mutually inverse single-valued reference properties.

2. A bidirectional many-to-many association is mapped to a pair of mutually inverse multi-valued reference properties, one in each of the two classes participating in the association. Again, in one of the two classes, the multi-valued reference property representing the (inverse) association is designated as a *derived property* that is automatically updated whenever the corresponding property in the other class (where the association is maintained) is updated. This transformation is illustrated in Figure 7.3.

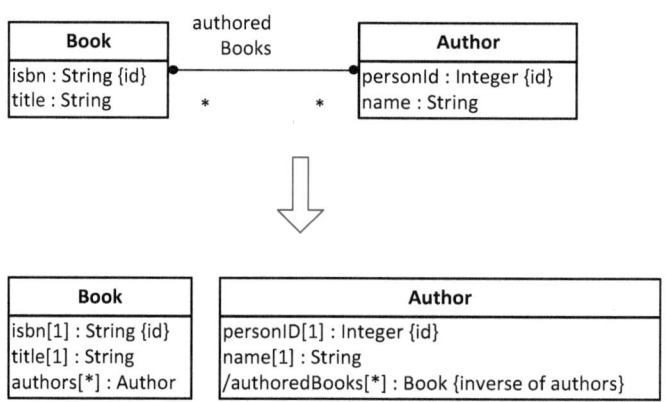

Figure 7.3: Turn a bidirectional many-to-many association into a master-slave pair of mutually inverse multi-valued reference properties.

7.2.4 The Resulting OO Class Model

After replacing both bidirectional associations with reference properties, we obtain the OO class model shown in 7.4.

Book
isbn[1] : String {id}
title[1] : String
year[1] : Integer
publisher[0..1] : Publisher
authors[*] : Author

Publisher
name[1] : String {id}
adress[1] : String
/publishedBooks[*] : Book {inverse of publisher}

Author
personId[1] : Integer {id}
name[1] : String
/authoredBooks[*] : Book {inverse of authors}

Figure 7.4: The OO class model with two pairs of mutually inverse reference properties.

Since books are entities that existentially depend on authors and possibly on publishers, and not the other way around, it's natural to maintain the master references in book objects, and consider the inverse references in publisher and author objects as derived (or 'slave') data. Therefore, we define publishedBooks and authoredBooks as derived inverse reference properties, which is indicated by their slash prefix in the OO class model.

The meaning of this OO class model can be illustrated by a sample data population for the three model classes involved:

Publisher

Name	Address	Published books
Bantam Books	New York, USA	0553345842
Basic Books	New York, USA	0465030793

Book

ISBN	Title	Year	Authors	Publisher
0553345842	The Mind's I	1982	1, 2	Bantam Books
1463794762	The Critique of Pure Reason	2011	3	
1928565379	The Critique of Practical Reason	2009	3	
0465030793	I Am A Strange Loop	2000	2	Basic Books

Author		
Author ID	**Name**	**Authored books**
1	Daniel Dennett	0553345842
2	Douglas Hofstadter	0553345842, 0465030793
3	Immanuel Kant	1463794762, 1928565379

Notice how Book records reference Publisher and Author records, and, vice versa, Publisher and Author records reference Book records.

8 Implementing Bidirectional Associations with Plain JS

In this chapter, we show

1. how to derive a JS class model from an OO class model with **derived inverse reference properties**,
2. how to code the JS class model in the form of JavaScript model classes,
3. how to write the view and controller code based on the model code.

8.1 Make a JavaScript Class Model

The starting point for making our JS class model is an OO class model with derived inverse reference properties like the one discussed above, which we present here again, for convenience:

Book
isbn[1] : String {id}
title[1] : String
year[1] : Integer
publisher[0..1] : Publisher
authors[*] : Author

Publisher
name[1] : String {id}
adress[1] : String
/publishedBooks[*] : Book {inverse of publisher}

Author
personId[1] : Integer {id}
name[1] : String
/authoredBooks[*] : Book {inverse of authors}

Notice that the model contains two derived inverse reference properties: Publisher::/publishedBooks and Author::/authoredBooks. Each of them is linked to a master property, from which it is derived. Consequently, each of them represents a pair of mutually inverse reference properties corresponding to a bidirectional association.

Compared to making JS class models with unidirectional associations, the only new issue is:

1. Add a «get» stereotype to all derived inverse reference properties, implying that they have an implicit getter, but no setter. They are implicitly set whenever their inverse master reference property is updated.

This concerns the two derived inverse reference properties Publisher::/publishedBooks and Author::/authoredBooks. Thus, we get the following JavaScript class model:

https://doi.org/10.1515/9783110500325-009

Book
«get/set» isbn[1] : string {id}
«get/set» title[1] : string
«get/set» year[1] : number(int)
«get/set» publisher[0..1] : Publisher
«get/set» authors[*] : Author
checkIsbn(in isbn : String) : ConstraintViolation
checkIsbnAsId(in isbn : String) : ConstraintViolation
checkIsbnAsIdRef(in isbn : String) : ConstraintViolation
checkTitle(in title : String) : ConstraintViolation
checkYear(in year : Integer) : ConstraintViolation
checkPublisher(in p : Publisher) : ConstraintViolation
checkAuthor(in author : Author) : ConstraintViolation
addAuthor(in author : Author)
removeAuthor(in author : Author)
toString() : string
toRecord() : Object

Publisher
«get/set» name[1] : string {id}
«get/set» adress[1] : string
«get» publishedBooks[*] : Book {inverse of publisher}
checkName(in n : String) : ConstraintViolation
checkNameAsId(in n : String) : ConstraintViolation
checkNameAsIdRef(in n : String) : ConstraintViolation
checkAddress(in a : String) : ConstraintViolation
toString() : string
toRecord() : Object

Author
«get/set» personId[1] : number(int) {id}
«get/set» name[1] : string
«get» authoredBooks[*] : Book {inverse of authors}
checkPersonId(in pId : Integer) : ConstraintViolation
checkPersonIdAsId(in pId : Integer) : ConstraintViolation
checkPersonIdAsIdRef(in pId : Integer) : ConstraintViolation
checkName(in name : String) : ConstraintViolation
toString() : string
toRecord() : Object

8.2 Write the Model Code

The JS class model can be directly coded for getting the code of the model layer of our JavaScript frontend app.

8.2.1 New Issues

Compared to the *unidirectional association app*, we have to deal with a number of new technical issues:

1. We define the derived inverse reference properties, like Publisher::/publishedBooks, without a *check* operation and without a *set* operation.
2. We also have to take care of maintaining the derived inverse reference properties by maintaining the derived (sets of) inverse references that form the collection value of a derived inverse reference property. This requires in particular that
   1. whenever the value of a ***single-valued*** master reference property is ***initialized or updated*** with the help of a setter (such as assigning a reference to a Publisher instance p to b.publisher for a Book instance b), an inverse reference has to be assigned or added to the corresponding value of the derived inverse reference property (such as adding b to p.publishedBooks); when the value of the master reference property is *updated* and the derived inverse reference property is *multi-valued*, then the obsolete inverse reference to the previous value of the single-valued master reference property has to be deleted;

2. whenever the value of an optional ***single-valued*** master reference property is ***unset*** (e.g. by assigning null to b.publisher for a Book instance b), the inverse reference has to be removed from the corresponding value of the derived inverse reference property (such as removing b from p.publishedBooks), if the derived inverse reference property is multi-valued, otherwise the corresponding value of the derived inverse reference property has to be unset or updated;

3. whenever a reference is ***added*** to the value of a ***multi-valued*** master reference property with the help of an add method (such as adding an Author reference a to b.authors for a Book instance b), an inverse reference has to be assigned or added to the corresponding value of the derived inverse reference property (such as adding b to a.authoredBooks);

4. whenever a reference is ***removed*** from the value of a ***multi-valued*** master reference property with the help of a remove method (such as removing a reference to an Author instance a from b.authors for a Book instance b), the inverse reference has to be removed from the corresponding value of the derived inverse reference property (such as removing b from a.authoredBooks), if the derived inverse reference property is multi-valued, otherwise the corresponding value of the derived inverse reference property has to be unset or updated;

5. whenever an object with a single reference or with multiple references as the value of a master reference property is ***destroyed*** (e.g., when a Book instance b with a single reference b.publisher to a Publisher instance p is destroyed), the derived inverse references have to be removed first (e.g., by removing b from p.publishedBooks).

Notice that when a new object is created with a single reference or with multiple references as the value of a master reference property (e.g., a new Book instance b with a single reference b.publisher), its setter or add method will be invoked and will take care of creating the derived inverse references.

8.2.2 Coding Summary

Code each class of the JS class model as an ES2015 class with implicit getters and setters (or, alternatively, as an ES5 constructor function with explicit setters):

1. Code the property checks in the form of class-level ('static') methods. Take care that all constraints of a property as specified in the JS class model are properly coded in the property checks.

2. For each single-valued property, code the specified getter and setter:
   1. In each setter, the corresponding property check is invoked and the property is only set/unset, if the check does not detect any constraint violation.
   2. **If the concerned property is the inverse of a derived reference property (representing a bidirectional association), make sure that the**

> setter also assigns/unsets (or adds/removes) the corresponding inverse reference to/from (the collection value of) the inverse property.

3. For each multi-valued property, code its add and remove operations, as well as the specified get/set operations:
   1. Code the add/remove operations as (instance-level) methods that invoke the corresponding property checks.
   2. Code the setter such that it invokes the add operation for each item of the collection to be assigned.
   3. **If the concerned property is the inverse of a derived reference property (representing a bidirectional association), make sure that the add/remove methods also assign/unset (or add/remove) the corresponding inverse reference to/from (the collection value of) the inverse property.**

4. Write the code of the serialization function `toString()` and the object-to-storage conversion function `toRecord()`. In the object-to-storage conversion of a publisher or author object with `toRecord()`, the derived properties `publishedBooks` and `authoredBooks` are not included since their information is redundant (it is derived from the `publisher` and `authors` properties of books).

5. Take care of deletion dependencies in the `destroy` method. **Make sure that when an object with a single reference or with multiple references as the value of a master reference property is destroyed, the derived inverse references are unset (or removed) first.**

These steps are discussed in more detail in the following sections.

8.2.3 Code Each Class of the JS Class Model

For instance, the `Publisher` class from the JS class model is coded in the following way:

```js
class Publisher {
  constructor ({name, address}) {
    this.name = name;
    this.address = address;
    // derived inverse reference property (inverse of Book::publisher)
    this._publishedBooks = {}; // initialize as an empty map
  }
  get name() {. . .}
  static checkName( n) {. . .}
  static checkNameAsId( n) {. . .}
```

```
    static checkNameAsIdRef( n) {. . .}
    set name( n) {. . .}
    get address() {. . .}
    static checkAddress( a) {. . .}
    set address( a) {. . .}
    toString() {. . .}
    toRecord() {. . .}
}
```

Notice that we have added the (derived) multi-valued reference property publishedBooks, but we do not assign it in the constructor function because it is a read-only property that is assigned implicitly when its inverse master reference property Book::publisher is assigned.

8.2.4 Code the Set Methods of Single-Valued Properties

Any setter for a reference property that is coupled to a derived inverse reference property (implementing a bidirectional association), now also needs to assign/add/ remove inverse references to/from the corresponding collection value of the inverse reference property. An example of such a setter is publisher in the Book class:

```
set publisher( p) {
  if (!p) { // the publisher reference is to be deleted
    // delete the inverse reference in Publisher::publishedBooks
    delete this._publisher.publishedBooks[ this._isbn];
    // unset the publisher property
    delete this._publisher;
  } else {
    // p can be an ID reference or an object reference
    const publisher_id = (typeof p !== "object") ? p : p.name;
    const constraintViolation = Book.checkPublisher( publisher_id);
    if (constraintViolation instanceof NoConstraintViolation) {
      if (this._publisher) {
        // delete the inverse reference in Publisher::publishedBooks
        delete this._publisher.publishedBooks[ this._isbn];
      }
      // create the new publisher reference
      this._publisher = Publisher.instances[ publisher_id];
      // add the new inverse reference to Publisher::publishedBooks
```

```
    this._publisher.publishedBooks[ this._isbn] = this;
  } else {
    throw constraintViolation;
  }
 }
}
```

8.2.5 Code the Add and Remove Operations

For any multi-valued reference property that is coupled to a derived inverse reference property, both the *add* and the *remove* method also have to assign/add/remove corresponding references to/from (the value set of) the inverse property.

For instance, for the multi-valued reference property Book::authors that is coupled to the derived inverse reference property Author:authoredBooks for implementing the bidirectional authorship association between Book and Author, the Book::addAuthor method is coded in the following way:

```
addAuthor( a) {
  // a can be an ID reference or an object reference
  const author_id = (typeof a !== "object") ? parseInt(a) : a.authorId;
  const validationResult = Book.checkAuthor( author_id);
  if (author_id && validationResult instanceof NoConstraintViolation) {
    // add the new author reference
    this._authors[author_id] = Author.instances[author_id];
    // automatically add the derived inverse reference
    this._authors[author_id].authoredBooks[this._isbn] = this;
  } else {
    throw validationResult;
  }
}
```

For the remove operation removeAuthor we obtain the following code:

```
removeAuthor( a) {
  // a can be an ID reference or an object reference
  const author_id = (typeof a !== "object") ? parseInt(a) : a.authorId;
  const validationResult = Book.checkAuthor( author_id);
  if (validationResult instanceof NoConstraintViolation) {
    // automatically delete the derived inverse reference
    delete this._authors[author_id].authoredBooks[this._isbn];
    // delete the author reference
```

```
      delete this._authors[author_id];
   } else {
      throw validationResult;
   }
}
```

8.2.6 Suppress the Storage of the Values of Derived Properties

In the object-to-storage conversion of a publisher or author object with toRecord(), the derived properties publishedBooks and authoredBooks are not included since their information is redundant (derived from the publisher and authors properties of books). For instance, the Author::toRecord function is coded in the following way:

```
toRecord() {
   var rec = {};
   // loop over all Author properties
   for (let p of Object.keys( this)) {
      // keep underscore-prefixed properties except "_authoredBooks"
      if (p.charAt(0) === "_" && p !== "_authoredBooks") {
         // remove underscore prefix
         rec[p.substr(1)] = this[p];
      }
   };
   return rec;
}
```

8.2.7 Take Care of Deletion Dependencies

When a Book instance b, with a single reference b.publisher to a Publisher instance p and multiple references b.authors to Author instances, is destroyed, the derived inverse references have to be removed first (e.g., by removing b from p.publishedBooks):

```
Book.destroy = function (isbn) {
   const book = Book.instances[isbn];
   if (book) {
   console.log( book.toString() + " deleted!");
   if (book.publisher) {
      // remove inverse reference from book.publisher
      delete book.publisher.publishedBooks[isbn];
```

```
  }
  // remove inverse references from all book.authors
  for (let authorID of Object.keys( book.authors)) {
    delete book.authors[authorID].authoredBooks[isbn];
  }
  // finally, delete book from Book.instances
  delete Book.instances[isbn];
} else {
  console.log(`There is no book with ISBN ${isbn} in the database!`);
  }
};
```

8.3 Exploit Inverse Reference Properties in the User Interface

In the *UI code* we can now exploit the inverse reference properties for more efficiently creating a list of inversely associated objects in the *Retrieve/List All* use
case. For instance, we can more efficiently create a list of all published books for
each publisher. However, we do not allow updating the set of inversely associated
objects in the *update object* use case (e.g. updating the set of published books in
the *update publisher* use case). Rather, such an update has to be done via updating
the master objects (in our example, the books) concerned.

8.3.1 Show Information About Published Books in *Retrieve/List All*

For showing information about published books in the *Retrieve/List All publishers*
use case, we can now exploit the derived inverse reference property publishedBooks:

```
pl.v.publishers.retrieveAndListAll = {
  setupUserInterface: function () {
    const tableBodyEl = document.querySelector("section#Publisher-
R>table>tbody");
    tableBodyEl.innerHTML = "";
    for (let key of Object.keys( Publisher.instances)) {
      const publisher = Publisher.instances[key];
      const row = tableBodyEl.insertRow(-1);
      // create list of books published by this publisher
      const listEl = util.createListFromMap( publisher.publishedBooks, "title");
      row.insertCell(-1).textContent = publisher.name;
```

```
      row.insertCell(-1).textContent = publisher.address;
      row.insertCell(-1).appendChild( listEl);
    }
    document.getElementById("Publisher-M").style.display = "none";
    document.getElementById("Publisher-R").style.display = "block";
  }
};
```

9 Implementing Bidirectional Associations with Java EE

In this chapter, we show

1. how to derive a Java ***Entity class model*** from an OO class model (that has been derived from an information design model),
2. how to code the Entity class model in the form of entity classes (representing *model classes*),
3. how to write the view and controller code based on the entity classes.

9.1 Make a Java Entity Class Model

The starting point for making a Java Entity class model is an OO class model with derived inverse reference properties like the one discussed above (in Figure 7.4), which we present here again, for convenience:

Book
isbn[1] : String {id}
title[1] : String
year[1] : Integer
publisher[0..1] : Publisher
authors[*] : Author

Publisher
name[1] : String {id}
adress[1] : String
/publishedBooks[*] : Book {inverse of publisher}

Author
personId[1] : Integer {id}
name[1] : String
/authoredBooks[*] : Book {inverse of authors}

Notice that the model contains two derived inverse reference properties: `Publisher::/publishedBooks` and `Author::/authoredBooks`. Each of them is linked to a master property, from which it is derived, by means of an *inverse-of* constraint. Consequently, each of them represents a pair of mutually inverse reference properties corresponding to a bidirectional association.

We now show how to derive a Java Entity class model from the OO class model:

1. Turn each class into a «Java Entity» class, making all properties private.
2. Replace the platform-independent datatype names of the OO class model with corresponding Java datatype classes (`Integer`, `Float`, etc.).
3. Add a «get/set» stereotype to all non-derived properties for indicating that they need getters and setters.
4. Add a «get» stereotype to all derived properties for indicating that they need getters, only.

https://doi.org/10.1515/9783110500325-010

5. For any reference property, depending on the functionality type of the association represented by it, add a corresponding keyword as property modifier. For the given OO class model, add the following property modifiers:
   - oneToMany to the derived reference property Publisher::/publishedBooks,
   - manyToOne to the reference property Book::publisher
   - manyToMany to the reference property Book::authors
   - manyToMany to the derived reference property Author::/authoredBooks
6. For any derived reference property designated as the inverse of another reference property, replace its *{inverse of . . . }* property modifier with a corresponding *{mappedBy="..."}* property modifier.
7. Create the required property constraint check operations.
8. Create an *add*, and a *remove* operation for each *multi-valued* property.

This leads to the following Java Entity class model:

«Java Entity»
Publisher
«get/set» -name[1] : String {id} «get/set» -adress[1] : String «get» -/publishedBooks[*] : Book {oneToMany, mappedBy="publisher"}
+checkNameAsId(in n : String, in em : EntityManager) : ConstraintViolation +toString() : String +retrieveAll(in em : EntityManager) : List<Publisher> +create(in em : EntityManager, in name : String, in address : String) +update(in em : EntityManager, in name : String, in address : String) +delete(in em : EntityManager, in name : String)

«Java Entity»
Book
«get/set» -isbn[1] : String {id} «get/set» -title[1] : String «get/set» -year[1] : Integer «get/set» -publisher[0..1] : Publisher {manyToOne} «get/set» -authors[*] : Author {manyToMany}
+checkIsbnAsId(in isbn : String) : ConstraintViolation +addAuthor(in author : Author) +removeAuthor(in author : Author) +toString() : string +...()

«Java Entity»
Author
«get/set» -personId[1] : Integer {id} «get/set» -name[1] : String «get» -/authoredBooks[*] : Book {manyToMany, mappedBy="authors"}
+checkPersonIdAsId(in pId : Integer, in em : EntityManager) : ConstraintViolation +toString() : String +...()

9.2 Write the Model Code

The Java Entity class model can be directly coded for getting the model layer code of our Java back-end app.

9.2.1 New Issues

Compared to the *unidirectional association app* discussed before, we have to deal with a number of new technical issues:

1. In the *model code* you now have to take care of maintaining the derived inverse reference properties by maintaining the derived (sets of) inverse references that form the values of a derived inverse reference property. This requires in particular that

    1. whenever the value of a **single-valued** master reference property is **initialized or updated** with the help of a setter (such as assigning a reference to an Publisher instance p to b.publisher for a Book instance b), an inverse reference has to be assigned or added to the corresponding value of the derived inverse reference property (such as adding b to p.publishedBooks); when the value of the master reference property is *updated* and the derived inverse reference property is *multi-valued*, then the obsolete inverse reference to the previous value of the single-valued master reference property has to be deleted;

    2. whenever the value of an optional **single-valued** master reference property is **unset** (e.g. by assigning null to b.publisher for a Book instance b), the inverse reference has to be removed from the corresponding value of the derived inverse reference property (such as removing b from p.publishedBooks), if the derived inverse reference property is multi-valued, otherwise the corresponding value of the derived inverse reference property has to be unset or updated;

    3. whenever a reference is **added** to the value of a **multi-valued** master reference property with the help of an add method (such as adding an Author reference a to b.authors for a Book instance b), an inverse reference has to be assigned or added to the corresponding value of the derived inverse reference property (such as adding b to a.authoredBooks);

    4. whenever a reference is **removed** from the value of a **multi-valued** master reference property with the help of a remove method (such as removing a reference to an Author instance a from b.authors for a Book instance b), the inverse reference has to be removed from the corresponding value of the derived inverse reference property (such as removing b from a.authoredBooks), if the derived inverse reference property is multi-valued,

otherwise the corresponding value of the derived inverse reference property has to be unset or updated;

5.   whenever an object with a single reference or with multiple references as the value of a master reference property is ***destroyed*** (e.g., when a Book instance b with a single reference b.publisher to a Publisher instance p is destroyed), the derived inverse references have to be removed first (e.g., by removing b from p.publishedBooks).

Notice that when a new object is created with a single reference or with multiple references as the value of a master reference property (e.g., a new Book instance b with a single reference b.publisher), its setter or add method will be invoked and will take care of creating the derived inverse references.

2.   In the *UI code* we can now exploit the inverse reference properties for more efficiently creating a list of inversely associated objects in the *list objects* use case. For instance, we can more efficiently create a list of all published books for each publisher.

9.2.2 Summary

1.   Code each class of the Java Entity class model as a corresponding entity class.
2.   Code an {id} property modifier with the JPA annotation @Id.
3.   Code any property modifier denoting the functionality type of a reference property, such as {manyToOne}, with the corresponding JPA annotation, such as @ManyToOne.
4.   Code the integrity constraints specified in the model with the help of Java Bean Validation annotations (or custom validation annotations).
5.   Code the getters and setters as well as the *add* and *remove* methods for multivalued properties.
6.   Code the create, retrieve, update and delete storage management operations as class-level methods.
7.   Take care of the inverse relation management in the create and update methods.

These steps are discussed in more detail in the following sections.

9.2.3 Code Each Class of the Java Entity Class Model

In the Publisher class, we add the publishedBooks property and we use the @OneToMany annotation corresponding to @ManyToOne from the Book class, representing the inverse relation:

```
@Entity
public class Publisher {

    . . .

    @OneToMany( fetch=FetchType.EAGER, mappedBy="publisher")
    private Set<Book> publishedBooks;

    . . .

}
```

The `mappedBy` parameter of the `@OneToMany` annotation of the `Publisher::` `publishedBooks` property specifies the property that implements the `@ManyToOne` relation in the `Book` class:

```
@Entity
public class Book {

    . . .

    @ManyToOne( fetch=FetchType.EAGER)
    @JoinColumn( name="PUBLISHER_NAME")
    private Publisher publisher;

    . . .

}
```

In the `Author` class we add the `authoredBooks` property with the `@ManyToMany` annotation corresponding to `@ManyToMany` from the `Book` class representing the inverse relation:

```
@Entity
public class Author {

    . . .

    @ManyToMany( fetch=FetchType.EAGER, mappedBy="authors")
    private Set<Book> authoredBooks;

    . . .

}
```

The `mappedBy` attribute of the `@ManyToMany` annotation for `authoredBooks` reference property of the `Author` class specifies the name of the inverse reference property in the `Book` class:

```
@Entity. . .
public class Book {

    . . .

    @ManyToMany( fetch=FetchType.EAGER)
    @JoinTable( name="books_authors",
```

```
    joinColumns = {@JoinColumn( name="BOOK_ISBN")},
    inverseJoinColumns = {@JoinColumn( name="AUTHOR_PERSONID")})
 private Set<Author> authors;
 . . .
}
```

We also use the @JoinTable annotation to specify the join table name for the *Many-To-Many* relation and the corresponding colum names for the join table, e.g., the table is books_authors and the columns are named BOOK_ISBN and AUTHOR_PERSONID.

9.2.4 Code the Setter Operations

Any setter for a reference property that is coupled to a derived inverse reference property (implementing a bidirectional association), now also needs to assign/add/remove inverse references to/from the corresponding value (set) of the inverse property. An example of such a setter is the following setPublisher method:

```
public class Book {
  . . .
  public void setPublisher( Publisher publisher) {
    // remove the book reference from publisher.publishedBooks
    if (this.publisher != null) {
      this.publisher.removePublishedBook( this);
    }
    // add the book to publisher.publishedBooks
    if (publisher != null) {
      publisher.addPublishedBook( this);
    }
    this.publisher = publisher;
  }
}
```

9.2.5 Code the Add and Remove Operations

For any multi-valued reference property that is coupled to a derived inverse reference property, both the *add* and the *remove* method also have to assign/add/remove corresponding references to/from (the value set of) the inverse property.

For instance, for the multi-valued reference property `Book::authors` that is coupled to the derived inverse reference property `Author:authoredBooks` for implementing the bidirectional authorship association between `Book` and `Author`, the addAuthor method is coded in the following way:

```
public class Book {
   . . .
   public void addAuthor( Author author) {
     if (this.authors == null) {
       this.authors = new HashSet<  Author>();
     }
     if (!this.authors.contains( author)) {
       // add the new author reference
       this.authors.add( author);
       // add the derived inverse reference
       author.addAuthoredBook( this);
     }
   }
}
```

For the remove operation removeAuthor we obtain the following code:

```
public class Book {
   . . .
   public void removeAuthor( Author author) {
     if (this.authors != null && author != null &&
         this.authors.contains( author)) {
       // delete the author reference
       this.authors.remove( author);
       // delete the derived inverse reference
       author.removeAuthoredBook( this);
     }
   }
}
```

Remember, for a Java `Collection`, such as `Set` or `List`, the contains method compares two objects by using the equals method of the objects. For example, for using the contains method over a `Set<Authors>`, such as `publishedBooks`, in the Author class we implement the following equals method (two authors are equal if their personId property values are equal):

```
public class Author {
    . . .
    @Override
    public boolean equals( Object obj) {
      if (obj instanceof Author) {
        Author author = (Author) obj;
        return ( this.personId.equals( author.personId));
      } else return false;
    }
    . . .
}
```

9.2.6 Take Care of Deletion Dependencies

When a Book instance b, with a single reference b.publisher to a Publisher instance p and multiple references b.authors to Author instances, is destroyed,
the derived inverse references have to be removed first (e.g., by removing b from
p.publishedBooks). This is accomplished by calling the set methods for the single
and multi-valued properties with a null parameter, e.g., b.setPublisher(null)
and b.setAuthors(null) within the Book.delete method:

```
public class Book {
    . . .
    public static void delete( EntityManager em,
        UserTransaction ut, String isbn) throws Exception {
      ut.begin();
      Book b = em.find( Book.class, isbn);
      b.setPublisher( null);
      b.setAuthors( null);
      em.remove( b);
      ut.commit();
    }
}
```

In the same way, we have to take care of deleting the references to Book instances
when deleting a Publisher or an Author instance:

```
public class Author {
    . . .
    public static void delete( EntityManager em,
       UserTransaction ut, Integer personId) throws Exception {
    ut.begin();
    Author a = em.find( Author.class, personId);
    a.setAuthoredBooks( null);
    em.remove( a);
    ut.commit();
    }
}
```

And, likewise,

```
public class Publisher {
    public static void delete( EntityManager em,
        UserTransaction ut, String name) throws Exception {
    ut.begin();
    Publisher p = em.find( Publisher.class, name);
    p.setPublishedBooks( null);
    em.remove( p);
    ut.commit();
    }
}
```

9.2.7 Entity Managers and Cached Entities

Unfortunately, JPA does not provide automatic maintenance of derived inverse references. According to the Java Persistence Wiki, we have to implement the (direct and inverse) relations management within set/add/remove methods:

> *A common problem with bidirectional relationships is the application updates one side of the relationship, but the other side does not get updated, and becomes out of sync. In JPA, as in Java in general, it is the responsibility of the application or the object model to maintain relationships. If your application adds to one side of a relationship, then it must add to the other side. This is commonly resolved through add or set methods in the object model that handle both sides of the relationships, so the application code does not need to worry about it. There are two ways to go about this: you can either add the relationship maintenance code to only one side of the relationship, and only use the setter from that side (such as making the other side protected), or add it to both sides and ensure you avoid an infinite loop.*

We have used an entity manager for each controller class. Every entity manager maintains a set of cached entities which can be "shared" with other entity managers by using the merge method. In our example code, as part of the create and update methods of each model class, we have to merge the updated entities that belong to another entity manager. For example, in the Book.create method, we need to merge the new book's publisher, managed by the PublisherController's entity manager, and all its authors, managed by the AuthorController's entity manager:

```
public class Book {
    public static void create( EntityManager em,
        UserTransaction ut,
        String isbn, String title, Integer year,
        Publisher publisher, Set<Author> authors)
        throws Exception {
      ut.begin();
      Book book = new Book( isbn, title, year,
          publisher, authors);
      em.persist( book);
      if (publisher != null) {
        em.merge( publisher);
      }
      if (authors != null)
        for (Author a : authors) {
          em.merge( a);
      }
    }
    ut.commit();
    }
}
```

Without using merge, the publisher as well as all author instances from the authors list, do not represent references to the originally cached entities, and are not going to retain our changes. For more details, please check the Java Persistence Documentation related to this matter.

It is also possible to disable the JPA caching, so the entities are reloaded from the database for every new instance, e.g., when EntityManager.find method is called. This can be achieved by adding the following line in the persistence.xml file:

```
<property name="eclipselink.cache.shared.default" value="false"/>
```

The above configuration works for eclipselink implementation and it may be different for other API implementations. Notice that disabling entity caching is not recommended without a serious reason, since it degrades the app's performance and may produce unpredicted behavior in some cases, such as when using @SessionScoped managed entities.

9.3 Exploiting Derived Inverse Reference Properties in the User Interface

We can now exploit the derived inverse reference properties Publisher:: publishedBooks and Author::authoredBooks for more efficiently creating a list of associated books in the *retrieve/list all publishers* and *retrieve/list all authors* use cases.

9.3.1 Show Information About Published Books in *Retrieve/List All*

For showing information about published books in the *retrieve/list all publishers* use case, we can now exploit the derived inverse reference property publishedBooks:

```
<ui:composition template="/WEB-INF/templates/page.xhtml">
  <ui:define name="content">
    <h:dataTable value="#{publisherController.publishers}" var="p">
      . . .
      <h:column>
        <f:facet name="header">Published books</f:facet>
        <h:outputText value="#{p.publishedBooks}" escape="false"
          converter="pl.m.converter.BookListConverter"/>
      </h:column>
    </h:dataTable>
    <h:button value="Back" outcome="index" />
  </ui:define>
</ui:composition>
```

In the case of unidirectional associations, for the case of the *retrieve/list all books* use case, we have used a method in the Book model class, i.e., getAuthorNames(), which returns a comma-separated list of author names as a string:

```
public class Book {
  . . .
  public String getAuthorNames() {
    String result = "";
    int i = 0, n = 0;
    if (this.authors != null) {
      n = this.authors.size();
      for (Author author : this.authors) {
```

```
      result += author.getName();
      if (i < n - 1) {
        result += ", ";
      }
      i++;
    }
  }
  return result;
  }
}
```

This makes sense in the case of a book, since the number of authors is in general limited to a small number. However, a Publisher may have a large number of published books. As a better alternative to our string serialization, we can use a JSF converter class which allows us to present the list of authors in a custom way. In our case, we choose to present it as list of names, where every name is presented on a separate line. For this, we implement the pl.m.converter.BookListConverter class and we annotate it with **@FacesConverter** as follows:

```
@FacesConverter( value="pl.m.converter.BookListConverter")
public class BookListConverter implements Converter {
  @Override
  public Object getAsObject( FacesContext context,
      UIComponent component, String value) {
    return null; // this method is not needed
}
@Override
public String getAsString( FacesContext context,
    UIComponent component, Object value) {
  String result = "";
  int i=0, n=0;
  if (value == null) {
    return null;
  } else if (value instanceof Set<?>) {
    n = ((Set<Book>) value).size();
    for (Book b : (Set<Book>) value) {
      result += b.getTitle();
      if (i < n-1) {
        result += "<br />";
      }
      i++;
```

```
    }
    return result;
  }
  return null;
  }
}
```

Then, we use the `converter` attribute in the facelet to specify that our converter class, e.g., `pl.m.converter.BookListConverter`, has to be used when the respective view component needs to be rendered:

```
<h:column>
  <f:facet name="header">Published books</f:facet>
  <h:outputText value="#{p.publishedBooks}" escape="false"
    converter="pl.m.converter.BookListConverter"/>
</h:column>
```

Since the serialization text contains HTML elements, i.e., `<br />` to produce HTML new lines, we have to specify the **@escape="false"** attribute, otherwise < and > will be replaced with the corresponding `&lt;` and `&gt;` entities.

The main advantage of using JSF converters is that we do not mix model code with view specific code, so our model classes remain clean and later, if we like to replace JSF with another UI technology, then our model classes remain unchanged, and we just need to take care of a corresponding converter for the new technology.

9.4 Run the App and Get the Code

For running your application, you may first have to stop your Tomcat/TomEE server (with `bin/shutdown.bat` for Windows or `bin/shutdown.sh` for Linux). Next, download and unzip our ZIP archive file containing all the source code of the application and also the ANT script file that you have to edit (modify the `server.folder` property value). Now, execute the following command in your console or terminal:

```
ant deploy -Dappname=BidirectionalAssociationApp
```

Finally, start your Tomcat web server (by using `bin/startup.bat` for Windows OS or `bin/startup.sh` for Linux). Please be patient, this can take some time depending on the speed of your computer. Finally, open a web browser and type:

```
http://localhost:8080/BidirectionalAssociationApp/WebContent/views/app/
index.xhtml
```

10 Special Topics on Associations

10.1 Part-Whole Associations

A part-whole association represents a relationship between a part type and a whole type. Its instances are part-whole relationships between two objects where one of them is a part of the other (the whole). The UML makes a distinction between two kinds of part-whole associations: *aggregation* and *composition*. While these two terms are defined in a pretty precise, albeit unsatisfactory, way in the UML, many software developers have a different interpretation following a terminological tradition of the C++ programming community where, unlike the parts of an 'aggregation', the parts of a 'composition' cannot exist independently of the composite that references them.

We follow the UML and improve their definition of composition by introducing a distinction between two kinds of compositions: those with *separable* parts and those with *inseparable* parts.

10.1.1 Aggregation

An aggregation is a special form of a part-whole association, where the parts of a whole can be shared with other wholes. For instance, we can model an aggregation between the classes DegreeProgram and Course, as shown in the following diagram, since a course is part of a degree program and a course can be shared among two or more degree programs (e.g. an engineering degree could share a C programming course with a computer science degree).

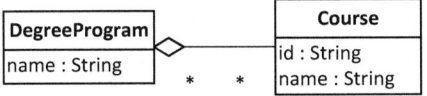

However, the concept of an aggregation with **shareable parts** doesn't mean much, really, so it does not have any implications on how to code the association and many developers therefore prefer not to use the white diamond in their class diagrams, but just model a plain association instead. The UML spec says: "Precise semantics of shared aggregation varies by application area and modeler".

The **multiplicity** of an aggregation's association end at the whole side may be any number (*) because a part may belong to, or **shared** among, any number of wholes.

https://doi.org/10.1515/9783110500325-011

10.1.2 Composition

It's amazing how much confusion exists about the distinction between the part-whole association concepts *aggregation* and *composition*. The main problem is the widespread misunderstanding (even among expert software developers and among the authors of UML) that the concept of composition implies a life-cycle dependency between the whole and its parts such that the parts cannot exist without the whole. But this view ignores the fact that there are also cases of part-whole associations with non-shareable parts where the parts can be detached from and survive the destruction of the whole.

In the UML specification document, the definition of the term "composition" has always implied non-shareable parts, but it has not been clear what is the defining characteristic of "composition", and what is merely an optional characteristic. Even in the UML version 2.5 (as of 2015), after an attempt to improve the definition of the term "composition", it remains still ambiguous and doesn't provide any guidance how to model part-whole associations with non-shareable parts where the parts can be detached from, and survive the destruction of, the whole as opposed to the case where the parts cannot be detached and are destroyed together with the whole. They say:

> If a composite object is deleted, all of its part instances that are objects are deleted with it.

But at the same time they also say:

> A part object may be removed from a composite object before the composite object is deleted, and thus not be deleted as part of the composite object.

This confusion points to an incompleteness of the UML definition, which does not account for life-cycle dependencies between components and composites. It's therefore important to understand how the UML definition can be enhanced, e.g. by introducing a UML stereotype for «inseparable» compositions, or by introducing a constraint keyword inseparable for characterizing the association end at the component side.

As Martin Fowler has explained, the main issue for characterizing composition relationships is that "an object can only be the part of one composition relationship". This is also explained in the blog post UML Composition vs Aggregation vs Association by G. Bellekens. In addition to this defining characteristic of a composition (to have **exclusive**, or **non-shareable**, parts), a composition may also come with a life-cycle dependency between the composite and its components. In fact, there are two kinds of such dependencies:

1. Whenever a component **must always be attached** to a composite, or, in other words, when it has a **mandatory composite**, as expressed by the "exactly one" multiplicity at the composite side of the composition line, then it must either be re-used in (or re-attached to) another composite, or destroyed, when its current composite is destroyed. This is exemplified by the composition between Person and Heart, shown in the diagram below. A heart is either destroyed or transplanted to another person, when its owner has died.

2. Whenever a component ***must not be detached*** from its composite, or, in other words, when it is ***inseparable***, then, and only then, the component has to be destroyed, when its composite is destroyed. An example of such a composition with inseparable parts is the composition between Person and Brain.

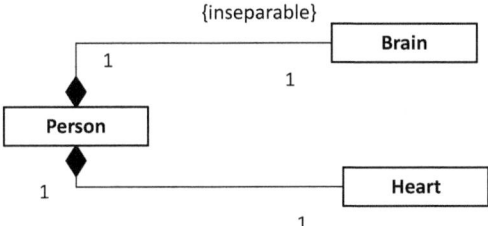

In summary, the life-cycle dependency created by inseparable parts only applies to specific cases of composition, but not in general. It is, therefore, not a defining characteristic. The UML spec states: "A part may be removed from a composite instance before the composite instance is deleted, and thus not be deleted as part of the composite instance."

When such a life-cycle dependency applies, it represents a special form of *Existential Dependency*, which implies the CASCADE deletion policy discussed in Section 1.2.

In the example of a Car-Engine composition, as shown in the following diagram, it's clearly the case that the engine can be detached from the car before the car is destroyed, in which case the engine is not destroyed and can be re-used. This is implied by the ***zero or one*** multiplicity at the composite side of the composition line.

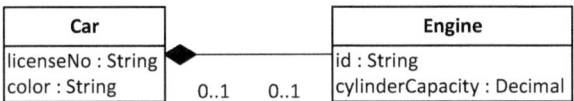

The ***multiplicity*** of a composition's association end at the composite side is either 1 or 0..1, depending on the fact if components have a mandatory composite or not. Of course, the fact that a component is inseparable implies that it has a mandatory composite, and consequently the composite's multiplicity must be 1.

10.1.3 Example

As an example of a part-whole association, we consider the association between textbooks and their chapters. Normally, a chapter of a textbook cannot be reused in another book without revisions (e.g., because it may reference other parts of the textbook). Also, it doesn't make sense to allow having textbook chapters that are not part of a textbook. We therefore model this association as an inseparable composition, as shown in the following diagram.

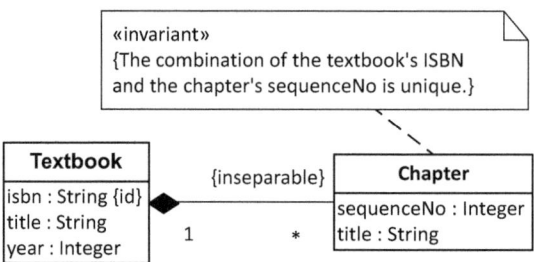

An object class representing an inseparable component type, like Chapter, does not need to have a standard identifier attribute because there is no need for inseparable component objects to be referenced independently of their composite object. For referencing inseparable component objects, a composite key that is composed of the primary key of the composite type and a suitable (relatively unique) attribute of the component type is used. For instance, a textbook chapter is referenced by a combination of the textbook's ISBN and the chapter's sequence number.

Since Chapter objects, as inseparable components of Textbook objects, cannot continue to exist when their Textbook object ceases to exist, we need to use the CASCADE deletion policy, requiring to delete all associated chapters along with deleting a textbook, in the implementation of the *Delete Textbook* operation.

An inseparable component type does not require its own CRUD data management user interfaces. Rather, all its CRUD operations are provided within the data management user interfaces of its composite type. For instance, creating, retrieving, updating and deleting textbook chapters is done within the user interfaces for managing textbook data.

10.2 Association Classes

An association class is a class that represents an association.

Recall that simple associations are eliminated in an OO class model by turning them into reference properties of the involved object classes, as shown in Section 1.7. But whenever an association has attributes, it cannot be eliminated and has to be turned into a class in an OO class model.

As an example, consider the association *Reservation* between the object types *Book* and *Person*, allowing to express facts like "the book with ISBN 3627921105 has a reservation by the person with ID 4701199 on 2020-08-22". Since it has an attribute *date*, this association is modeled as an association class in an information design model, as shown in the following class diagram:

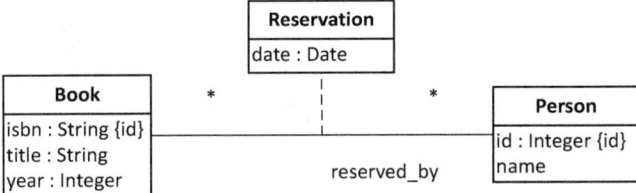

In an OO class model, which is the basis for coding the model classes of an app, association classes are turned into ordinary classes, with reference properties that reference the involved object classes. For instance, the association class *Reservation* is transformed into the following OO model class:

Reservation
book : Book
reserved_by : Person
date : Date

11 Bidirectional Associations Practice Projects

All projects include the following tasks:

1. Make an *OO class model* derived from the given information design model. Hint: replace associations with corresponding reference properties.
2. Make a *JavaScript class model* or a *Java Entity class model* derived from the OO class model. Hint: add check and setter methods.
3. Code your JavaScript class model or Java Entity class model, following the provided guidelines.

Make sure that your pages comply with the XML syntax of HTML5, and that your JavaScript code complies with our Coding Guidelines and is checked with JSHint (http://www.jshint.com).

11.1 Assign Directors/Actors to Movies and Movies to Directors/ Actors

This project is based on the information design model below. The app from the previous assignment is to be extended by adding *derived inverse reference properties* for implementing the bidirectional associations. This is achieved by adding the multi-valued reference properties directedMovies and playedMovies to the model class Person, both with range Movie.

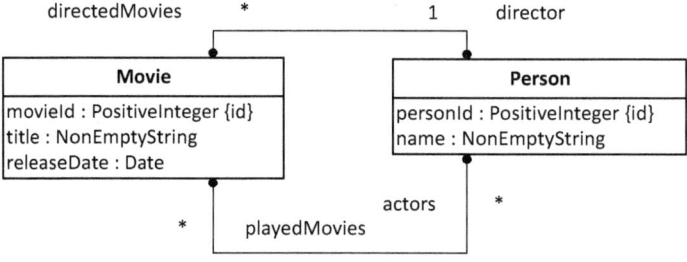

You can use the following sample data for testing your app:

Movies

Movie ID	Title	Release date	Director	Actors
1	Pulp Fiction	1994-05-12	1	5, 6
2	Dangerous Liaisons	1988-12-16	2	7, 5
3	Inglourious Basterds	2009-05-20	1	9, 1

https://doi.org/10.1515/9783110500325-012

People

Person ID	Name	Directed movies	Played movies
1	Quentin Tarantino	1, 3	3
2	Stephen Frears	2	
5	Uma Thurman		1, 2
6	John Travolta		1
7	Keanu Reeves		2
9	Brad Pitt		3

More movie data can be found at the IMDb website.

11.2 Assign Cities to a Country and Members to an Organization, and Vice Versa

This project is based on the information design model shown below. The corresponding app from the previous assignments is to be extended by adding the possibility to manage data about *international organizations*, with countries as *members*, and about *cities*, as *capitals* and *headquarter locations*. This is achieved by adding corresponding model classes InternationalOrganization and City, and the following unidirectional associations:

1. a many-to-many association between InternationalOrganization and Country assigning zero or more countries as the **members** of an international organization, and, inversely, zero or more international organizations to a country,
2. a one-to-many association between Country and City assigning zero or many cities to a country and, inversely, exactly one country to a city.

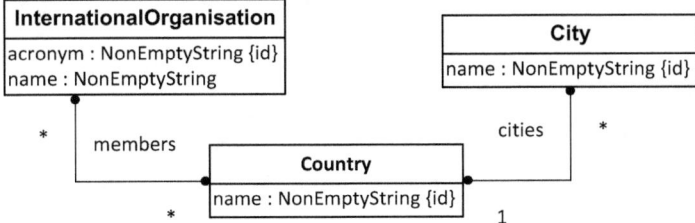

You can use the following sample data for testing your app:

International organizations

Acronym	Name	Members
UN	United Nations	Germany, France, Russia
WHO	World Health Organization	Germany, France, Russia
NATO	North Atlantic Treaty Organization	Germany, France

Countries

Name	Cities	International organizations
Germany	Berlin, Hamburg, Frankfurt	UN, WHO, NATO
France	Marseille, Lyon, Paris	UN, WHO, NATO
Russia	Moscow, Novosibirsk	UN, WHO

Cities

Name	Country
Berlin	Germany
Frankfurt	Germany
Hamburg	Germany
Lyon	France
Marseille	France
Moscow	Russia
Novosibirsk	Russia
Paris	France

More data about countries can be found at the CIA World Factbook website.

Part II: **Inheritance in Class Hierarchies**

Whenever an app has to manage the data of a larger number of object types, there may be various **subtype** (inheritance) relationships between some of the object types. Subtypes and inheritance are important elements of information models. Software applications have to implement them in a proper way, typically as part of their *model* layer within a *model-view-controller* (MVC) architecture. Unfortunately, application development frameworks do often not provide much support for dealing with class hierarchies and inheritance.

https://doi.org/10.1515/9783110500325-013

12 Subtyping and Inheritance

The concept of a *subtype*, or *subclass*, is a fundamental concept in natural language, mathematics, and informatics. For instance, in English, we say that *a bird is an animal*, or the class of all birds is a *subclass* of the class of all animals. In linguistics, the noun "bird" is a *hyponym* of the noun "animal".

An object type may be specialized by subtypes (for instance, *Bird* is specialized by *Parrot*) or generalized by supertypes (for instance, *Bird* and *Mammal* are generalized by *Animal*). Specialization and generalization are two sides of the same coin.

A subtype **inherits** all features from its supertypes. When a subtype inherits attributes, associations and constraints from a supertype, this means that these features need not be repeatedly rendered for the subtype in the class diagram, but the reader of the diagram has to understand that all features of a supertype also apply to its subtypes.

When an object type has more than one direct supertype, we have a case of **multiple inheritance**, which is common in conceptual modeling, but prohibited in many object-oriented programming languages, such as Java and C#, which only allow **class hierarchies** with a unique direct supertype for each object type.

12.1 Introducing Subtypes by Specialization

A new object type may be introduced by specialization whenever it represents a special case of another object type. We illustrate this for our example model where we want to capture text books and biographies as special cases of books. This means that text books and biographies also have an ISBN, a title and a publishing year, but in addition they have further features such as the attribute subjectArea for text books and the attribute about for biographies. Consequently, in Figure 12.1, we introduce the object types TextBook and Biography by specializing the object type Book, that is, as subtypes of Book.

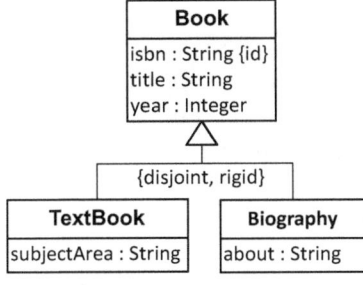

Figure 12.1: The object type Book with two subtypes: TextBook and Biography.

https://doi.org/10.1515/9783110500325-014

When specializing an object type, we define additional features for the newly added subtype. In many cases, these additional features are more specific properties. For instance, in the case of TextBook specializing Book, we define the additional attribute subjectArea. In some programming languages, such as in Java, it is therefore said that the subtype *extends* the supertype.

However, we can also specialize an object type without defining additional properties or operations/methods, but by defining additional constraints.

12.2 Introducing Supertypes by Generalization

We illustrate generalization with the example shown in Figure 12.2.

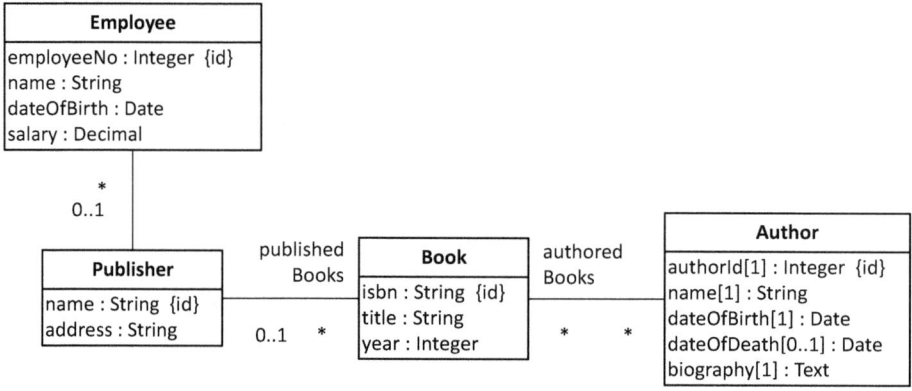

Figure 12.2: The object types Employee and Author share several attributes.

After adding the object type Employee we notice that Employee and Author share a number of attributes due to the fact that both employees and authors are people, and *being an employee* as well as *being an author* are **roles** played by people. So, we may generalize these two object types by adding a joint supertype Person, as shown in the diagram of Figure 12.3.

When generalizing two or more object types, we move those features that are shared by them to the newly added supertype where they are centralized. In the case of Employee and Author, this set of shared features consists of the attributes name, dateOfBirth and dateOfDeath. In general, shared features may include attributes, associations and constraints.

Notice that since in an information design model, each top-level class needs to have a standard identifier, in the new class Person we have declared the standard identifier attribute personId, which is inherited by all subclasses. Therefore, we

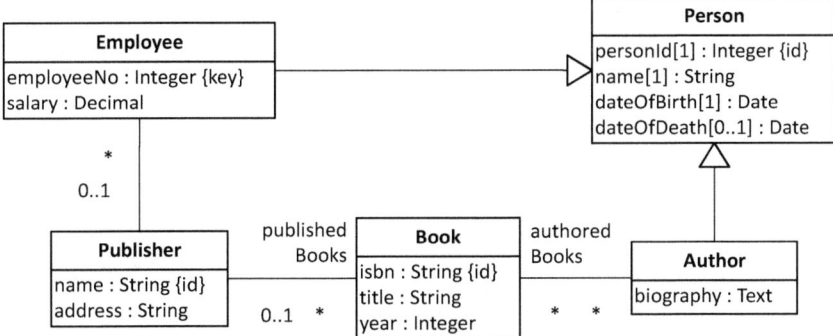

Figure 12.3: The object types Employee and Author are generalized by the common supertype Person.

have to reconsider the attributes that had been declared to be standard identifiers in the subclasses before the generalization. In the case of Employee, we had declared the attribute employeeNo as a standard identifier. Since the employee number is an important business information item, we have to keep this attribute, even if it is no longer the standard identifier. Because it is still an alternative identifier (a "key"), we define a *uniqueness* constraint for it with the constraint keyword key.

In the case of Author, we had declared the attribute authorId as a standard identifier. Assuming that this attribute represents a purely technical, rather than business, information item, we dropped it, since it's no longer needed as an identifier for authors. Consequently, we end up with a model which allows to identify employees either by their employee number or by their personId value, and to identify authors by their personId value.

We consider the following extension of our original example model, shown in Figure 12.4, where we have added two class hierarchies:
1. the disjoint (but incomplete) segmentation of Book into TextBook and Biography,
2. the overlapping and incomplete segmentation of Person into Author and Employee, which is further specialized by Manager.

12.3 Intension versus Extension

The **intension** of an object type is given by the set of its features, including attributes, associations, constraints and operations.

The **extension** of an object type is the set of all objects instantiating the object type. The extension of an object type is also called its *population*.

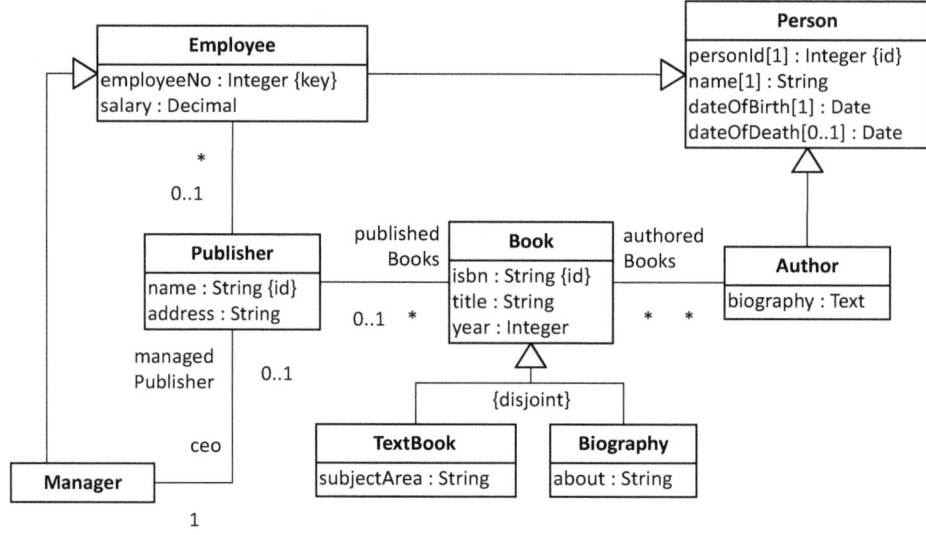

Figure 12.4: An information model with two class hierarchies.

We have the following duality: while all features of a supertype are included in the intensions, or feature sets, of its subtypes (intensional inclusion), all instances of a subtype are included in the extensions, or instance sets, of its supertypes (extensional inclusion). This formal structure has been investigated in formal concept analysis.

Due to the intension/extension duality we can specialize a given type in two different ways:

1. By **extending the type's intension** through adding features in the new subtype (such as adding the attribute subjectArea in the subtype TextBook).
2. By **restricting the type's extension** through adding a constraint (such as defining a subtype MathTextBook as a TextBook where the attribute subjectArea has the specific value "Mathematics").

Typical OO programming languages, such as Java and C#, only support the first possibility (specializing a given type by extending its intension), while XML Schema and SQL99 also support the second possibility (specializing a given type by restricting its extension).

12.4 Type Hierarchies

A *type hierarchy* (or *class hierarchy*) consists of two or more types, one of them being the *root* (or *top-level*) type, and all others having at least one direct supertype.

When all non-root types have a unique direct supertype, the type hierarchy is a *single-inheritance hierarchy*, otherwise it's a *multiple-inheritance hierarchy*. For instance, in Figure 12.5 below, the class Vehicle is the root of a single-inheritance hierarchy, while Figure 12.6 shows an example of a multiple-inheritance hierarchy, due to the fact that AmphibianVehicle has two direct superclasses: LandVehicle and WaterVehicle.

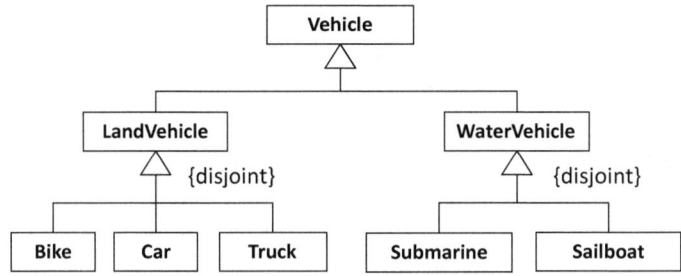

Figure 12.5: A class hierarchy having the root class Vehicle.

The simplest case of a class hierarchy, which has only one level of subtyping, is called a *generalization set* in UML, but may be more naturally called **segmentation**. A segmentation is **complete**, if the union of all subclass extensions is equal to the extension of the superclass (or, in other words, if all instances of the superclass instantiate some subclass). A segmentation is **disjoint**, if all subclasses are pairwise disjoint (or, in other words, if no instance of the superclass instantiates more than one subclass). Otherwise, it is called *overlapping*. A complete and disjoint segmentation is a **partition**.

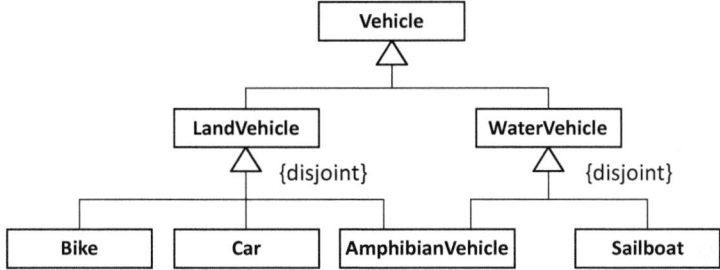

Figure 12.6: A multiple inheritance hierarchy.

In a class diagram, we can express these constraints by annotating the shared generalization arrow with the keywords *complete* and *disjoint* enclosed in braces. For instance, the annotation of a segmentation with {complete, disjoint} indicates that it is a partition. By default, whenever a segmentation does not have any annotation, like the segmentation of Vehicle into LandVehicle and WaterVehicle in Figure 12.6 above, it is {incomplete, overlapping}.

An information model may contain any number of class hierarchies.

12.5 Kinds and Roles

In order to better understand the different categories of object types and subtypes in natural language statements about the real world and in information models, we can distinguish between *sortal* and non-sortal, and between *rigid* and non-rigid object types, as proposed by Giancarlo Guizzardi in his theory of object type categories presented in Chapter 4 of Ontological foundations for structural conceptual models.

An object type is **sortal** if it has a uniform identity condition for its instances. Such a condition defines the property (or set of properties) that no two instances can have in common, without being the same object. An example of a sortal object type is Person since all its instances (people) are identifiable by a set of properties related to their birth (born when, where and to whom). Book is an example of a non-sortal object type because it contains instances (e.g., textbooks and self-published novels) that are identified in different ways.

An object type is **rigid** if its instances cannot cease to be of that type without ceasing to exist (or altering their identity). Person is an example of a rigid object type, while Employee is not rigid. A segmentation is called *rigid* if all segment subclasses are rigid.

A **kind** is a rigid sortal object type. Examples of kinds are TextBook and Person. A **role** is a sortal object type R classifying all instances of a kind K that participate in a relationship (of a certain type A) with an instance of an object type O. Notice that R is a non-rigid subtype of K since its instances do not cease to exist when they happen to cease instantiating R because they no longer participate in a relationship of type A with an instance of type O.

For instance, Employee is an example of a role since it is a sortal object type classifying all instances of Person that participate in an employment relationship with an instance of type Enterprise.

12.6 The *Class Hierarchy Merge* Design Pattern

Consider the simple class hierarchy of the design model in Figure 12.1 above, showing a disjoint segmentation of the class Book. In such a case, whenever there is only one level (or there are only a few levels) of subtyping and each subtype has only one (or a few) additional properties, it's an option to re-factor the class hierarchy by merging all the additional properties of all subclasses into an expanded version of the root class such that these subclasses can be dropped from the model, leading to a simplified model.

This *Class Hierarchy Merge* design pattern comes in two forms. In its simplest form, the segmentations of the original class hierarchy are **disjoint**, which allows to use a **single-valued** category attribute for representing the specific category of each instance of the root class corresponding to the unique subclass instantiated by it. When the segmentations of the original class hierarchy are not disjoint, that is, when at least one of them is **overlapping**, we need to use a **multi-valued** category attribute for representing the set of types instantiated by an object. We only discuss the simpler case of *Class Hierarchy Merge* re-factoring for disjoint segmentations, where we take the following re-factoring steps:

1. Add an **enumeration datatype** that contains a corresponding enumeration literal for each segment subclass. In our example, we add the enumeration datatype BookCategoryEL.
2. Add a category attribute to the root class with this enumeration as its range. The category attribute is mandatory [1], if the segmentation is complete, and optional [0..1], otherwise. In our example, we add a category attribute with range BookCategoryEL to the class Book. The category attribute is optional because the segmentation of Book into TextBook and Biography is incomplete.
3. Whenever the segmentation is **rigid**, we designate the category attribute as **frozen**, which means that it can only be assigned once by setting its value when creating a new object, but it cannot be changed later.
4. Move the properties of the segment subclasses to the root class, and make them **optional**. We call these properties, which are typically listed below the category attribute, **segment properties**. In our example, we move the attributes subjectArea from TextBook and about from Biography to Book, making them *optional*, that is [0..1].
5. Add a constraint (in an invariant box attached to the expanded root class rectangle) enforcing that the optional subclass properties have a value if and only if the instance of the root class instantiates the corresponding category. In our example, this means that an instance of Book is of category "TextBook" if and only if its attribute subjectArea has a value, and it is of category "Biography" if and only if its attribute about has a value.
6. Drop the segment subclasses from the model.

In the case of our example, the result of this design re-factoring is shown in Figure 12.7 below. Notice that the constraint (or "invariant") represents a logical sentence where the logical operator keyword "IFF" stands for the logical equivalence operator "if and only if" and the property condition prop=undefined tests if the property prop does not have a value.

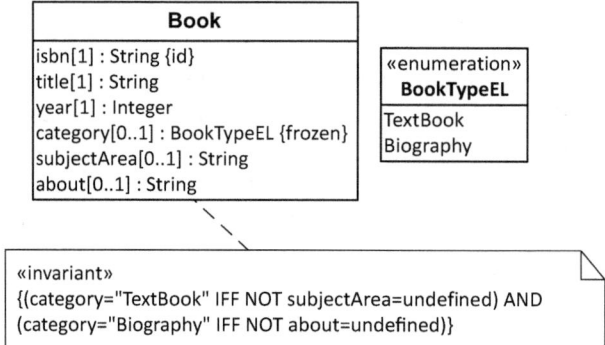

Figure 12.7: The result of applying the Class Hierarchy Merge design pattern.

12.7 Subtyping and Inheritance in Computational Languages

Subtyping and inheritance have been supported in *Object-Oriented Programming (OOP)*, in database languages (such as *SQL99*), in the XML schema definition language *XML Schema*, and in other computational languages, in various ways and to different degrees. At its core, subtyping in computational languages is about defining type hierarchies and the inheritance of features: properties, constraints and methods in OOP; table columns and constraints in SQL99; elements, attributes and constraints in XML Schema.

In general, it is desirable to have support for *multiple classification* and *multiple inheritance* in type hierarchies. Both language features are closely related and are considered to be advanced features, which may not be needed in many applications or can be dealt with by using workarounds.

Multiple classification means that an object has more than one direct type. This is mainly the case when an object plays multiple roles at the same time, and therefore directly instantiates multiple classes defining these roles.

Multiple inheritance is typically also related to role classes. For instance, a student assistant is a person playing both the role of a student and the role of an academic staff member, so a corresponding OOP class StudentAssistant inherits from both role classes Student and AcademicStaffMember. In a similar way, in our example model above, an AmphibianVehicle inherits from both role classes LandVehicle and WaterVehicle.

12.7.1 Subtyping and Inheritance in OOP

The minimum level of support for subtyping in OOP, as provided, for instance, by Java and C#, allows defining inheritance of properties and methods in single-inheritance hierarchies, which can be inspected with the help of an ***is-instance-of*** predicate that allows testing if a class is the direct or an indirect type of an object. In addition, it is desirable to be able to inspect inheritance hierarchies with the help of

1. a predefined instance-level property for retrieving ***the direct type of an object*** (or its *direct types*, if multiple classification is allowed);
2. a predefined type-level property for retrieving ***the direct supertype of a type*** (or its *direct supertypes*, if multiple inheritance is allowed).

A special case of an OOP language is JavaScript, which did originally not have an explicit language element for defining classes, but only for defining constructor functions. Due to its dynamic programming features, JavaScript allows using various code patterns for implementing classes, subtyping and inheritance. In modern JavaScript, starting from ES2015, defining a superclass and a subclass is straightforward. First, we define a base class, Person, with two properties, firstName and lastName:

```
class Person {
 constructor (first, last) {
// assign base class properties
  this.firstName = first;
  this.lastName = last;
 }
}
```

Then, we define a subclass, Student, with one additional property, studentNo:

```
class Student extends Person {
 constructor (first, last, studNo) {
// invoke constructor of superclass
  super( first, last);
// assign additional properties
  this.studentNo = studNo;
 }
}
```

Notice how the constructor of the superclass is invoked with super(first, last) for assigning the superclass properties.

12.7.2 Subtyping and Inheritance with XML Schema

In XML Schema, a subtype can be defined by *extending* or by *restricting* an existing complex type. While extending a complex type means **extending its intension** by adding elements or attributes, restricting a complex type means **restricting its extension** by adding constraints.

We can define a complex type Person and a subtype Student by extending Person in the following way:

```
<xs:complexType name="Person">
 <xs:attribute name="firstName" type="xs:string" />
 <xs:attribute name="lastName" type="xs:string" />
 <xs:attribute name="gender" type="GenderValue" />
</xs:complexType>
<xs:complexType name="Student">
 <xs:extension base="Person">
  <xs:attribute name="studentNo" type="xs:string" />
 </xs:extension>
</xs:complexType>
```

We can define a subtype FemalePerson by restricting Person in the following way:

```
<xs:complexType name="FemalePerson">
 <xs:restriction base="Person">
  <xs:attribute name="firstName" type="xs:string" />
  <xs:attribute name="lastName" type="xs:string" />
  <xs:attribute name="gender" type="GenderValue"
   use="fixed" value="f" />
 </xs:restriction>
</xs:complexType>
```

Notice that by fixing the value of the gender attribute to "f", we define a constraint that is only satisfied by the female instances of Person.

12.7.3 Subtyping and Inheritance with OWL

In the Web Ontology Language OWL, property definitions are separated from class definitions and properties are not single-valued, but multi-valued by default. Consequently, standard properties need to be declared as *functional*. Thus, we obtain the following code for expressing that Person is a class having the property name:

```
<owl:Class rdf:ID="Person"/>
<owl:DatatypeProperty rdf:ID="name">
  <rdfs:domain rdf:resource="#Person"/>
  <rdfs:range rdf:resource="xsd:string"/>
  <rdf:type rdf:resource="owl:FunctionalProperty"/>
</owl:DatatypeProperty>
```

OWL allows stating that a class is a subclass of another class in the following way:

```
<owl:Class rdf:ID="Student">
  <rdfs:subClassOf rdf:resource="#Person"/>
</owl:Class>
<owl:DatatypeProperty rdf:ID="studentNo">
  <rdfs:domain rdf:resource="#Student"/>
  <rdfs:range rdf:resource="xsd:string"/>
  <rdf:type rdf:resource="owl:FunctionalProperty"/>
</owl:DatatypeProperty>
```

For better usability, OWL should allow to define the properties of a class within a class definition, using the case of functional properties as the default case.

12.7.4 Representing Class Hierarchies with SQL Database Tables

A standard DBMS stores information (objects) in the rows of tables, which have been conceived as set-theoretic relations in classical *relational* database systems. The relational database language SQL is used for defining, populating, updating and querying such databases. But there are also simpler data storage techniques that allow to store data in the form of table rows, but do not support SQL. In particular, key-value storage systems, such as JavaScript's Local Storage API, allow storing a serialization of a *JS entity table* (a map of entity records) as the string value associated with the table name as a key.

While in the classical version of SQL (SQL92) there is no support for subtyping and inheritance, this has been changed in SQL99. However, the subtyping-related language elements of SQL99 have only been implemented in some DBMS, for instance in the open source DBMS *PostgreSQL*. As a consequence, for making a design model that can be implemented with various frameworks using various SQL DBMSs (including weaker technologies such as *MySQL* and *SQLite*), we cannot use the

SQL99 features for subtyping, but have to model inheritance hierarchies in database design models by means of plain tables and foreign key dependencies. This mapping from class hierarchies to relational tables (and back) is the business of **Object-Relational-Mapping** frameworks such as JPA Providers (like Hibernate), Microsoft's Entity Framework, or the Active Record approach of the Rails framework.

There are essentially three alternative approaches how to represent a class hierarchy with database tables:

1. **Single Table Inheritance** *(STI)* is the simplest approach, where the entire class hierarchy is represented by a single table, containing columns for all attributes of the root class and of all its subclasses, and named after the name of the root class.
2. **Table per Class Inheritance** *(TCI)* is an approach, where each class of the hierarchy is represented by a corresponding table containing also columns for inherited properties, thus repeating the columns of the tables that represent its superclasses.
3. **Joined Tables Inheritance** *(JTI)* is a more logical approach, where each segment subclass is represented by a corresponding table (subtable) connected to the table representing its superclass (supertable) via its primary key referencing the primary key of the supertable, such that the (inherited) properties of the superclass are not represented as columns in subtables.

Notice that the STI approach is closely related to the *Class Hierarchy Merge* design pattern discussed in Section 12.6 above. Whenever this design pattern has already been applied in the design model, or the design model has already been re-factored according to this design pattern, the class hierarchies concerned (their subclasses) have been eliminated in the design, and consequently also in the data model to be coded in the form of class definitions in the app's model layer, so there is no need anymore to map class hierarchies to single tables. Otherwise, the design model contains a class hierarchy that is implemented with a corresponding class hierarchy in the app's model layer, which would be mapped to database tables with the help of the STI approach.

We illustrate the use of these approaches with the help of two simple examples. The first example is the Book class hierarchy, which is shown in Figure 12.1 above. The second example is the class hierarchy of the Person roles Employee, Manager and Author, shown in the class diagram in Figure 12.8 below.

12.7.4.1 Single Table Inheritance

Consider the single-level class hierarchy shown in Figure 12.1 above, which is an incomplete disjoint segmentation of the class Book, as the design for the model classes of an MVC app. In such a case, whenever we have a model class hierarchy with

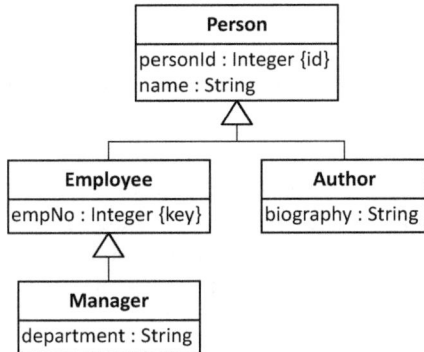

Figure 12.8: An information design model with a
Person roles hierarchy.

only one level (or only a few levels) of subtyping and each subtype has only a few
additional properties, it's preferable to use STI, so we model a single table containing columns for all attributes such that the columns representing additional attributes of segment subclasses ("segment attributes") are optional, as shown in the
SQL table model in Figure 12.9 below.

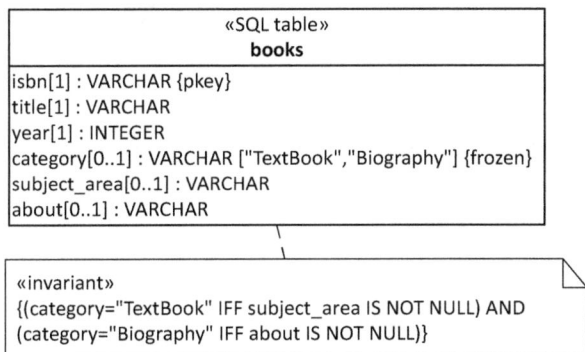

Figure 12.9: An SQL table model with a single table representing the Book class hierarchy.

It is a common approach to add a special *discriminator column* for representing the
category of each row corresponding to the subclass instantiated by the represented
object. Such a column would normally be string-valued, but constrained to one of
the names of the subclasses. If the DBMS supports enumerations, it could also be
enumeration-valued. We use the name category for the discriminator column,
which, in the case of our Book class hierarchy example, has a frozen value constraint since the textbook-biography segmentation is rigid.

Based on the category of a book, we have to enforce that if and only if it is
"TextBook", its attribute subjectArea has a value, and if and only if it is "Biography",
its attribute about has a value. This implied constraint is expressed in the invariant

box attached to the Book table class in the class diagram above, where the logical operator keyword "IFF" represents the logical equivalence operator "if and only if". It needs to be implemented in the database, e.g., with an SQL table CHECK clause or with SQL triggers.

When the given segmentation is disjoint, a single-valued enumeration attribute category is used for representing the information to which subclass an instance belongs. Otherwise, if it is non-disjoint, a multi-valued enumeration attribute categories is used for representing the information to which subclasses an instance belongs. Such an attribute can be implemented in SQL by defining a string-valued column for representing a set of enumeration codes or labels as corresponding string concatenations.

Consider the class hierarchy shown in Figure 12.8 above. With only three additional attributes defined in the subclasses Employee, Manager and Author, this class hierarchy can again be mapped with the STI approach, as shown in the SQL table model Figure 12.10 below.

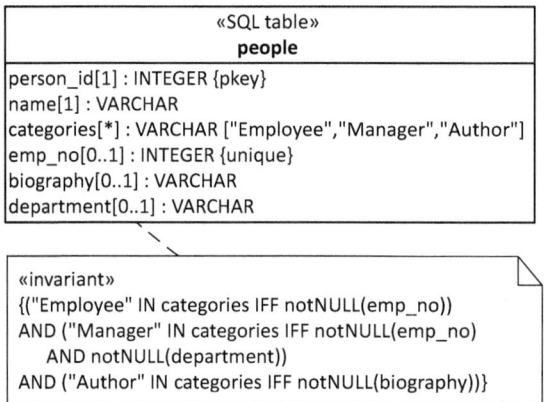

Figure 12.10: An STI table model representing the Person roles hierarchy.

Notice that now the discriminator column categories is multi-valued, since the segmentation of Person is not disjoint, but overlapping, implying that a Person object may belong to several categories. Notice also that, since a role segmentation (like *Employee, Manager, Author*) is not rigid, the discriminator column categories does not have a frozen value constraint.

An example of an admissible population for this model is the following:

people

person_id	name	categories	biography	emp_no	department
1001	Harry Wagner	Author, Employee	Born in Boston, MA, in 1956, . . .	21035	
1002	Peter Boss	Manager		23107	Sales
1003	Tom Daniels				
1077	Immanuel Kant	Author	Immanuel Kant (1724–1804) was a German philosopher . . .		

Notice that the Person table contains four different types of people:
1. A person, Harry Wagner, who is both an author (with a biography) and an employee (with an employee number).
2. A person, Peter Boss, who is a manager (a special type of employee), managing the Sales department.
3. A person, Tom Daniels, who is neither an author nor an employee.
4. A person, Immanuel Kant, who is an author (with a biography).

Pros of the STI approach: It leads to a faithful representation of the subtype relationships expressed in the original class hierarchy; in particular, any row representing a subclass instance (an employee, manager or author) also represents a superclass instance (a person).

Cons: (1) In the case of a multi-level class hierarchy where the subclasses have little in common, the STI approach does not lead to a good representation. (2) The structure of the given class hierarchy in terms of its elements (classes) is only implicitly preserved.

12.7.4.2 Table Per Class Inheritance
In a more realistic model, the subclasses of Person shown in Figure 12.8 above would have many more attributes, so the STI approach would be no longer feasible. In the TCI approach we get the SQL table model shown in Figure 12.11 below. A TCI model represents each concrete class of the class hierarchy as a table, such that each segment subclass is represented by a table that also contains columns for inherited properties, thus repeating the columns of the table that represents the superclass.

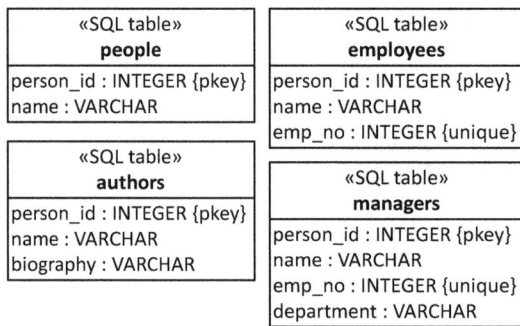

Figure 12.11: A TCI table model representing the Person roles hierarchy.

A TCI table model can be derived from the information design model by performing the following steps:

1. Replacing the standard ID property modifier {id} in all classes with {pkey} for indicating that the standard ID property is a *primary key*.
2. Replacing the singular (capitalized) class names (*Person, Author*, etc.) with pluralized lowercase table names (*people, authors*, etc.), and replacing camel case property names (*personId* and *empNo*) with lowercase underscore-separated names for columns (*person_id* and *emp_no*).
3. Adding a «table» stereotype to all class rectangles.
4. Replacing the platform-independent datatype names with SQL datatype names.
5. Dropping all generalization/inheritance arrows and adding all columns of supertables (such as person_id and name from people) to their subtables (authors and employees).

Each table would only be populated with rows corresponding to the direct instances of the represented class. An example of an admissible population for this model is the following:

people

personId	name
1003	Tom Daniels

authors

person_id	name	biography
1001	Harry Wagner	Born in Boston, MA, in 1956, . . .
1077	Immanuel Kant	Immanuel Kant (1724–1804) was a German philosopher . . .

(continued)

employees		
person_id	**name**	**emp_no**
1001	Harry Wagner	21035

managers			
person_id	**name**	**emp_no**	**department**
1002	Peter Boss	23107	Sales

Pros of the TCI approach: (1) The structure of the given class hierarchy in terms of its elements (classes) is explicitly preserved. (2) When the segmentations of the given class hierarchy are disjoint, TCI leads to memory-efficient non-redundant storage.

Cons: (1) The TCI approach does not yield a faithful representation of the subtype relationships expressed in the original class hierarchy. In particular, for any row representing a subclass instance (an employee, manager or author) there is no information that it represents a superclass instance (a person). Thus, the TCI database schema does not inform about the represented subtype relationships; rather, this meta-information, which is kept in the app's class model, is de-coupled from the database. (2) The TCI approach requires repeating column definitions, which is a form of schema redundancy. (3) The TCI approach may imply data redundancy whenever the segment subclasses overlap. In our example, authors can also be employees, so for any person in the overlap, we would need to duplicate the data storage for all columns representing properties of the superclass (in our example, this only concerns the property name).

12.7.4.3 Joined Tables Inheritance

For avoiding the data redundancy problem of TCI in the case of overlapping segmentations, we could take the JTI approach as exemplified in the SQL table model shown in Figure 12.12 below. This model connects tables representing subclasses (*subtables*) to tables representing their superclasses (*supertables*) by defining their primary key column(s) to be at the same time a foreign key referencing their supertable's primary key. Notice that foreign keys are visualized in the form of UML dependency arrows stereotyped with «fkey» and annotated at their source table side with the name of the foreign key column.

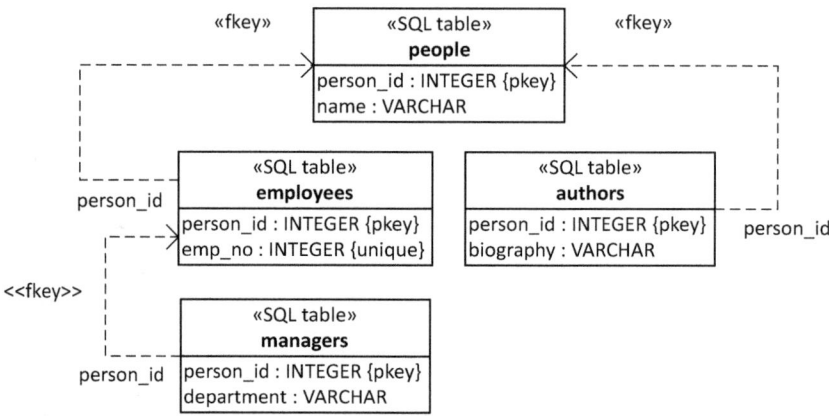

Figure 12.12: A JTI table model representing the Person roles hierarchy.

An example of an admissible population for this model is the following:

people

person_id	name
1001	Harry Wagner
1002	Peter Boss
1003	Tom Daniels
1077	Immanuel Kant

authors

person_id	biography
1001	Born in Boston, MA, in 1956, . . .
1077	Immanuel Kant (1724–1804) was a German philosopher . . .

employees

person_id	emp_no
1001	21035
1002	23107

managers

person_id	department
1002	Sales

Pros of the JTI approach: (1) Subtyping relationships and the structure of class hierarchies are explicitly preserved. (2) Data redundancy in the case of overlapping segmentations is avoided.

Cons: (1) The main disadvantage of the JTI approach is that for querying a subclass, *join queries* (for joining the segregated entity data) are required, which may create performance issues.

12.8 Quiz Questions

If you would like to look up the answers for the following quiz questions, you can check our discussion forum. If you don't find an answer in the forum, you may create a post asking for an answer to a particular question.

12.8.1 Question 1: Statements about a Class Hierarchy

Consider the following class model:

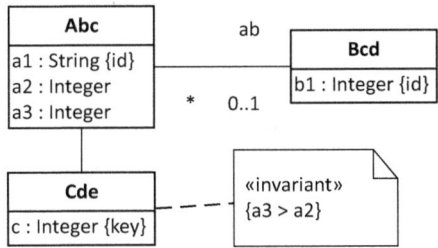

Which of the following statements are true? Select one or more:
1. ☐ All instances of Cde have a value for attribute a1.
2. ☐ The standard identifier of Cde is a1.
3. ☐ All instances of Cde may have an object reference ab referencing an object of type Bcd.
4. ☐ Direct instances of Abc may have a value for c.
5. ☐ For any object of type Abc the value of a3 must be greater than the value of a2.
6. ☐ For any object of type Cde the value of a3 must be greater than the value of a2.
7. ☐ The standard identifier of Cde is c.

12.8.2 Question 2: Class Hierarchy Merge

Consider the following class model:

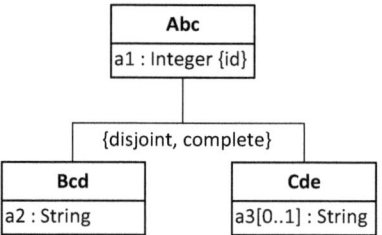

In the case of such a simple class hierarchy, we can use the *Class Hierarchy Merge* design pattern where the entire class hierarchy is merged into a single class. Which of the following models describes the correct implementation of the Class Hierarchy Merge design pattern for the given Abc class hierarchy? Select one:

1. O

Abc
a1[1] : Integer {id}
category[1] : AbcTypeEL
a2[1] : String
a3[0..1] : String

«enumeration» AbcTypeEL
Bcd
Cde

2. O

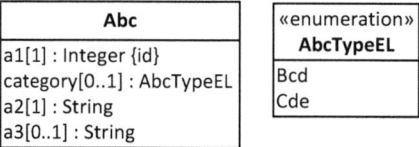

«enumeration» AbcTypeEL
Bcd
Cde

3. O

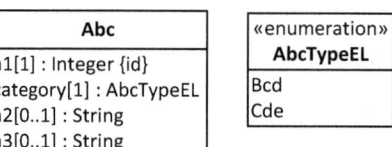

«enumeration» AbcTypeEL
Bcd
Cde

4. O

Abc
a1[1] : Integer {id}
a2[1] : String
a3[0..1] : String

13 Subtyping with Plain JS

In this chapter, we first explain the general approach to constructor-based subtyping in JavaScript before presenting two case studies based on fragments of the information model of our running example, the *Public Library* app, shown above.

In the first case study, we consider the single-level class hierarchy with root Book shown in Figure 12.1, which is an incomplete disjoint rigid segmentation. We use the *Class Hierarchy Merge* design pattern for re-factoring this simple class hierarchy to a single class that can be mapped to a persistent database table.

In the second case study, we consider the multi-level class hierarchy consisting of the Person roles Employee, Manager and Author, shown in Figure 12.8. The segmentation of Person into Employee and Author does not have any constraints, which means that it is incomplete, overlapping (non-disjoint) and non-rigid.

We use the *Class Hierarchy Merge* design pattern for re-factoring the simple Manager-is-Employee sub-hierarchy, and the *Joined Tables Inheritance* approach for mapping the Employee-and-Author-is-a-Person class hierarchy to a set of three database tables that are related with each other via foreign key dependencies.

In both case studies we show

1. how to derive a *JS class model*, and a corresponding *entity table model*, from the *information design model*,
2. how to code the JS class model in the form of *JS model classes*,
3. how to write the view and controller code based on the model code.

13.1 Subtyping with Constructor-Based Classes

Before the version ES2015, JavaScript did not have an explicit class concept and subtyping was not directly supported, so it had to be implemented with the help of certain code patterns providing two inheritance mechanisms: (1) inheritance of properties and (2) inheritance of methods.

As we have explained in Chapter 1 of Volume 1, classes can be defined in two alternative ways: **constructor-based** and **factory-based**. Both approaches have their own way of implementing inheritance.

https://doi.org/10.1515/9783110500325-015

We summarize the ES2015 code pattern for defining a superclass and a subclass in a constructor-based single-inheritance class hierarchy with the help of the following example:

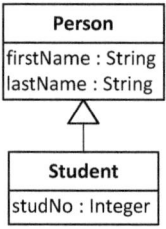

First, we define a base class, Person, with two properties, firstName and lastName, defined with getters and setters:

```
class Person {
    constructor ({first, last}) {
      // assign properties by invoking their setters
      this.firstName = first;
      this.lastName = last;
    }
    get firstName () {return this._firstName;}
    set firstName ( f ) {
      . . . // check constraints
      this._firstName = f;
    }
    get lastName () {return this._lastName;}
    set lastName ( l ) {
      . . . // check constraints
      this._lastName = l;
    }
}
```

Then, we define a subclass, Student, with one additional property, studNo:

```
class Student extends Person {
    constructor ({first, last, studNo}) {
      // invoke constructor of superclass
      super({first, last});
      // assign additional properties
      this.studNo = studNo;
    }
```

```
get studNo () {return this._studNo;}
set studNo ( sn) {
  . . . // check constraints
  this._studNo = sn;
}
}
```

Notice how the constructor of the superclass is invoked: with super({first, last}).

13.2 Case Study 1: Eliminating a Class Hierarchy

Simple class hierarchies can be eliminated by applying the *Class Hierarchy Merge* design pattern. The starting point for our case study is the simple class hierarchy shown in the information design model of Figure 12.1 above, representing a disjoint (but incomplete) rigid segmentation of Book into TextBook and Biography. This model is first simplified by applying the *Class Hierarchy Merge* design pattern, resulting in the following model:

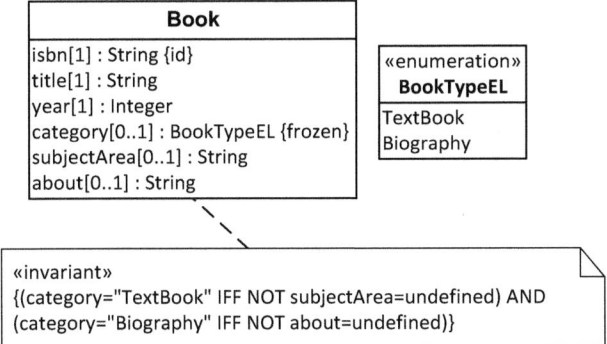

We can now derive a *JS class model* from this design model.

13.2.1 Make the JS Class Model

We make the JS class model in 3 steps:
1. Replace the platform-independent datatypes (used as the ranges of attributes and parameters) with JS datatypes. This includes the case of enumeration-valued attributes, such as category, which are turned into number-valued attributes restricted to the enumeration integers of the underlying enumeration type.

2. Decorate all properties with a «get/set» stereotype for indicating that they have implicit getters and setters.

3. Add property *check* functions, as described in Chapter 8 of Volume 1. The checkCategory function, as well as the checks of the segment properties need special consideration according to their implied semantics. In particular, a segment property's check function must ensure that the property can only be assigned if the category attribute has a value representing the corresponding segment. We explain this implied validation semantics in more detail below when we discuss how the JS class model is coded.

This leads to the JS class model shown in Figure 13.1, where the class-level ('static') methods are underlined:

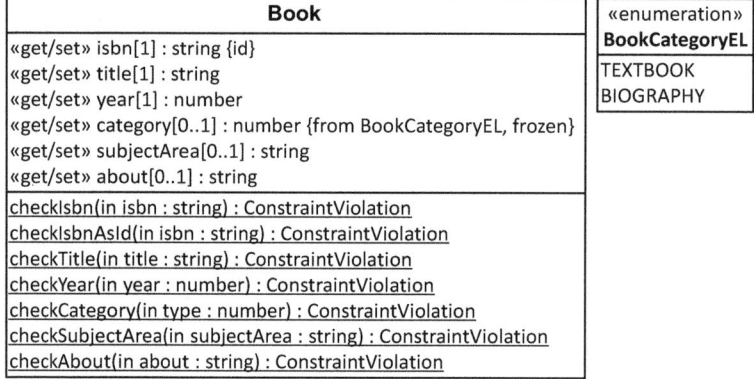

Figure 13.1: The JS class model of the merged Book class hierarchy.

13.2.2 New Issues

Compared to the enumeration app discussed in Chapter 11 of Volume 1, we have to deal with a number of new issues:

1. In the *model code* we have to take care of
    1. Adding the constraint violation class *FrozenValueConstraintViolation* to errorTypes.js.
    2. Coding the enumeration type to be used as the range of the category attribute (BookCategoryEL in our example).
    3. Coding the checkCategory function for the category attribute. In our example this attribute is *optional*, due to the fact that the Book segmentation is *incomplete*. If the segmentation, to which the *Class Hierarchy Merge* pattern is applied, is complete, then the category attribute is *mandatory*.

4. Coding the *check* functions for all segment properties such that they take the category as a second parameter for being able to test if the segment property concerned applies to a given instance.
5. Refining the serialization function toString() by adding a category case distinction (switch) statement for serializing only the segment properties that apply to the given category.
6. Implementing the *Frozen Value Constraint* for the category attribute in Book.update by updating the category of a book only if it has not yet been defined. This means it cannot be updated anymore as soon as it has been defined.

2. In the *UI code* we have to take care of
    1. Adding a "Special type" (or "Category") column to the display table of the "List all books" use case in books.html. A book without a special category will have an empty table cell, while for all other books their category will be shown in this cell, along with other segment-specific attribute values. This requires a corresponding switch statement in pl.v.books.retrieveAndListAll. setupUserInterface in the books.js view code file.
    2. Adding a "Special type" choice widget (typically, a selection list), and corresponding form fields for all segment properties, in the forms of the "Create book" and "Update book" use cases in books.html. Segment property form fields are only displayed when a corresponding book category has been selected. Such an approach of rendering specific form fields only on certain conditions is sometimes called *dynamic forms*.

13.2.3 Code the Model Classes of the JS Class Model

The JS class model can be directly coded for getting the code of the model classes of our JS front-end app.

13.2.3.1 Summary

1. Code the enumeration type BookCategoryEL to be used as the range of the category attribute with the help of the meta-class Enumeration, as explained in Chapter 11 of Volume 1.
2. Code the model class Book in the form of a JS class definition with get and set methods as well as static *check* functions.

These steps are discussed in more detail in the following sections.

13.2.3.2 Code the Enumeration Type BookCategoryEL

The enumeration type BookCategoryEL is coded with the help of our library meta-
class Enumeration at the beginning of the Book.js model class file in the following
way:

```
BookCategoryEL = new Enumeration([ "Textbook", "Biography"]);
```

13.2.3.3 Code the Model Class Book

We code the model class Book in the form of an ES2015 class definition where the
category attribute as well as the segment attributes subjectArea and about are optional, with getters, setters and static check functions for all properties:

```
class Book {
    constructor ({isbn, title, year, category, subjectArea, about}) {
        this.isbn = isbn;
        this.title = title;
        this.year = year;
        // optional properties
        if (category) this.category = category;
        if (subjectArea) this.subjectArea = subjectArea;
        if (about) this.about = about;
    }
    get isbn() {. . .}
    static checkIsbn( isbn) {. . .}
    static checkIsbnAsId( isbn) {. . .}
    set isbn( isbn) {. . .}
    get title() {. . .}
    static checkTitle( t) {. . .}
    set title( t) {. . .}
    get year() {. . .}
    static checkYear( y) {. . .}
    set year( y) {. . .}
    get category() {. . .}
    static checkCategory( c) {. . .}
    set category( c) {. . .}
    get subjectArea() {. . .}
    static checkSubjectArea( sA, cat) {. . .}
    set subjectArea( s) {. . .}
```

```
    get about() {. . .}
    static checkAbout( a, cat) {. . .}
    set about( a) {. . .}
}
```

Notice that the constructor function is defined with a single record parameter making use of the ES2015 feature of *function parameter destructuring*.

    We code the checkCategory and setCategory methods for the category attribute in the following way:

```
static checkCategory( c) {
    if (c === undefined || c === "") {
      return new NoConstraintViolation(); // category is optional
    } else if (!util.isIntegerOrIntegerString(c) || parseInt(c) < 1 ||
        parseInt(c) > BookCategoryEL.MAX) {
      return new RangeConstraintViolation(
          "Invalid value for category: "+ c);
    } else {
      return new NoConstraintViolation();
    }
};
set category( c) {
    var validationResult = null;
    if (this.category) { // already set/assigned
      validationResult = new FrozenValueConstraintViolation(
          "The category cannot be changed!");
    } else {
      validationResult = Book.checkCategory( c);
    }
    if (validationResult instanceof NoConstraintViolation) {
       this._category = parseInt( c);
    } else {
      throw validationResult;
    }
}
```

While the getters for segment properties (in this example: subjectArea and about) follow the standard pattern, their checks and setters have to make sure that the property applies to the category of the instance being checked. This is achieved by checking a combination of a property value and a category, as in the following example:

```
static checkSubjectArea( sA, c) {
  if (c === BookCategoryEL.TEXTBOOK && !sA) {
    return new MandatoryValueConstraintViolation(
        "A subject area must be provided for a textbook!");
  } else if (c !== BookCategoryEL.TEXTBOOK && sA) {
    return new ConstraintViolation("A subject area must not " +
        "be provided if the book is not a textbook!");
  } else if (sA && (typeof(sA) !== "string" || sA.trim() === "")) {
    return new RangeConstraintViolation(
        "The subject area must be a non-empty string!");
  } else {
    return new NoConstraintViolation();
  }
}
```

In the serialization function `toString`, we serialize the category attribute and the segment properties in a `switch` statement:

```
toString() {
  var bookStr = "Book{ ISBN:"+ this.isbn +", title:"+
      this.title +", year:"+ this.year;
  switch (this.category) {
  case BookCategoryEL.TEXTBOOK:
    bookStr += ", textbook subject area:"+ this.subjectArea;
    break;
  case BookCategoryEL.BIOGRAPHY:
    bookStr += ", biography about: "+ this.about;
    break;
  }
  return bookStr + "}";
};
```

In the update method of a model class, we only set a property if it is to be updated, that is, if there is a corresponding argument slot with a value that is different from the old property value. In the special case of a `category` attribute with a *Frozen Value Constraint*, we need to make sure that it can only be updated, along with an accompanying set of segment properties, if it has not yet been assigned. Thus, in the `Book.update` method, we perform the special test if `book.category === undefined` for handling the special case of an initial assignment, while we handle updates of the segment properties subjectArea and about in a more standard way:

```
Book.update = function ({isbn, title, year,
    category, subjectArea, about}) {
  const book = Book.instances[isbn],
      objectBeforeUpdate = util.cloneObject( book);
  var noConstraintViolated=true, updatedProperties=[];
  try {
    . . .
    if (category && book.category !== category) {
      book.category = category;
      updatedProperties.push("category");
    } else if (category === "" && "category" in book) {
      throw FrozenValueConstraintViolation(
          "The book category cannot be unset!");
    }
    if (subjectArea && book.subjectArea !== subjectArea) {
      book.subjectArea = subjectArea;
      updatedProperties.push("subjectArea");
    }
    if (about && book.about !== about) {
      book.about = about;
       updatedProperties.push("about");
    }
  } catch (e) {
      . . .
  }
  . . .
};
```

13.2.4 Write the View and Controller Code

The app's user interface (UI) consists of a start page that allows navigating to data management pages (in our example, to books.html). Such a data management page contains 5 sections: *manage books, list and retrieve all books, create book, update book* and *delete book*, such that only one of them is displayed at any time (by setting the CSS property display:none for all others).

13.2.4.1 Summary

We have to take care of handling the category attribute and the segment properties subjectArea and about both in the "Retrieve and list all books" use case as well as in the "Create book" and "Update book" use cases by

1. Adding a segment information column (with heading "Category") to the display table of the "Retrieve and list all books" use case in books.html.
2. Adding a "Category" selection field, and input fields for all segment properties, in the forms of the "Create book" and "Update book" use cases in books.html. The form fields for segment properties are only displayed, when a corresponding book category has been selected.

13.2.4.2 Add a Segment Information Column in *Retrieve/List All*

We add a "Special type" column to the display table of the "List all books" use case in books.html:

```
<table id="books">
 <thead><tr><th>ISBN</th><th>Title</th><th>Year</th><th>Category</th>
</tr></thead>
 <tbody></tbody>
</table>
```

A book without a special category will have an empty table cell in this column, while for all other books their category will be shown in this column, along with other category-specific information. This requires a corresponding switch statement in pl.v.books.retrieveAndListAll.setupUserInterface in the view/books.js file:

```
if (book.category) {
  switch (book.category) {
  case BookCategoryEL.TEXTBOOK:
    row.insertCell(-1).textContent = book.subjectArea + " textbook";
    break;
  case BookCategoryEL.BIOGRAPHY:
    row.insertCell(-1).textContent = "Biography about "+ book.about;
    break;
  }
}
```

13.2.4.3 Add a *Category* Selection Field in *Create* and *Update*

In both use cases, we need to allow selecting a special category of book ('textbook' or 'biography') with the help of a selection field, as shown in the following HTML fragment:

```
<div class="field">
<label>Category: <select name="category"></select></label>
</div>
<div class="field Textbook"><!-- conditional field -->
<label>Subject area: <input type="text" name="subjectArea" /></label>
</div>
<div class="field Biography"><!-- conditional field -->
<label>About: <input type="text" name="about" /></label>
</div>
```

Notice that we have added "Textbook" and "Biography" as additional values of the class attribute of the segment field container elements. This supports the rendering and un-rendering of "Textbook" and "Biography" form fields, depending on the value of the category attribute.

In the handleCategorySelectChangeEvent handler, segment property form fields are only displayed, with pl.v.app.displaySegmentFields, when a corresponding book category has been selected:

```
pl.v.books.handleCategorySelectChangeEvent = function (e) {
  var formEl = e.currentTarget.form,
      categoryIndexStr = formEl.category.value;
  if (categoryIndexStr) {
    pl.v.app.displaySegmentFields( formEl, BookCategoryEL.labels,
        parseInt( categoryIndexStr) + 1);
  } else {
    pl.v.app.undisplayAllSegmentFields( formEl, BookCategoryEL.labels);
  }
};
```

Recall that the category selection list contains a no-selection option "———" with the empty string as its return value, and a list of options formed by the enumeration labels of BookCategoryEL.labels such that their value is the corresponding array index (starting with 0) as a string. Consequently, the variable categoryIndexStr has either the value "" (empty string) or one of "0", "1", "2", etc.

13.3 Case Study 2: Implementing a Class Hierarchy

Whenever a class hierarchy is more complex, we cannot simply eliminate it, but have to implement it (1) in the app's model code, (2) in the underlying database and (3) in its user interface.

The starting point for our case study is the design model shown in Figure 12.8 above. In the following sections, we derive a *JS class model* and a *JS entity table model* from the design model. The entity table model is used as a design for the object-to-storage mapping that we need for storing the objects of our app with the browsers' Local Storage technology.

13.3.1 Make a JS Class Model

We design the *model classes* of our example app with the help of a *JS class model* that we derive from the *design model* by essentially leaving the generalization arrows as they are and just adding *get/set* methods and static *check* functions to each class. However, in the case of our example app, it is natural to apply the *Class Hierarchy Merge* design pattern (discussed in Section 12.6) to the single-subclass-segmentation of Employee for simplifying the class model by eliminating the Manager subclass. This leads to the model shown in Figure 13.2 below. Notice that a Person may be an Employee or an Author or both.

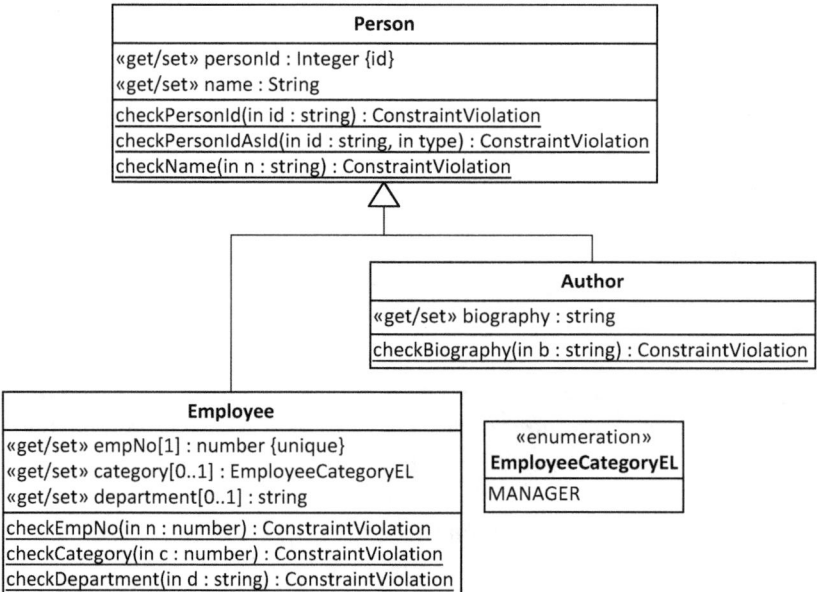

Figure 13.2: The JS class model of the Person roles class hierarchy.

13.3.2 Make a JS Entity Table Model

Since we use the browsers' *Local Storage* as the persistent storage technology for our example app, we have to deal with simple key-value storage. For each design model class with a singular (capitalized) name `Entity`, we use its pluralized lower-case name `entities` as the corresponding table name and as a key such that its associated string value is obtained by serializing the object collection `Entity.instances` with the help of the `JSON.stringify` method.

We design a set of suitable JS entity tables in the form of a *JS entity table model* that we derive from the information design model. We have to make certain choices how to organize our data store and how to derive a corresponding entity table model.

The first choice to make concerns using either the *Single Table Inheritance (STI)*, the *Table per Class Inheritance (TCI)* or the *Joined Tables Inheritance (JTI)* approach, which are introduced in Section 12.7.4. In the STI approach, a segmentation (or an entire class hierarchy) is represented with a single table, containing columns for all attributes of all classes involved, as shown in the example model of Figure 13.3.

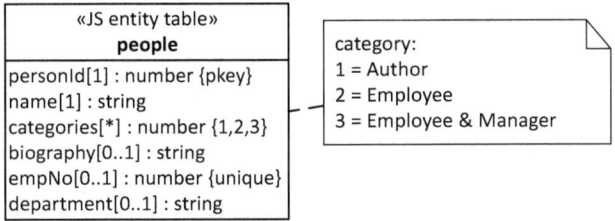

Figure 13.3: An STI model of the `Person` roles class hierarchy.

Since the given segmentation is non-disjoint, a multi-valued enumeration attribute `categories` is used for representing the information to which subclasses an instance belongs.

Using the STI approach is feasible for the given example, since the role hierarchy does not have many levels and the segment subclasses do not add many attributes. But, in a more realistic example, we would have a lot more attributes in the segment subclasses of the given role hierarchy. The STI approach is not really an option for representing a multi-level role hierarchy. However, we may choose it for representing the single-segment class hierarchy `Manager-is-subclass-of-Employee`.

For simplicity, and because the browsers' *Local Storage* does not support foreign keys as required by JTI, we choose the TCI approach, where we obtain a separate table for each class of the `Person` segmentation, but without foreign keys. Our choices result in the model shown in Figure 13.4 below, which has been derived from the design model shown in Figure Figure 12.8 by

1. Merging the `Manager` subclass into its superclass `Employee`, according to the *Class Hierarchy Merge* design pattern described in Section 12.6.
2. Replacing the standard ID property modifier {id} of the `personId` attribute of `Person`, `Author` and `Employee` with {pkey} for indicating that the attribute is a *primary key*.
3. Replacing the singular (capitalized) class names (*Person, Author* and *Employee*) with pluralized lowercase table names (*people, authors* and *employees*).
4. Adding the «JS entity table» stereotype to all class rectangles (`people`, `authors` and `employees`).
5. Replacing the platform-independent datatype names with JS datatype names.
6. Dropping all generalization/inheritance arrows and adding all attributes of supertables (`personId` and `name`) to their subtables (`authors` and `employees`).

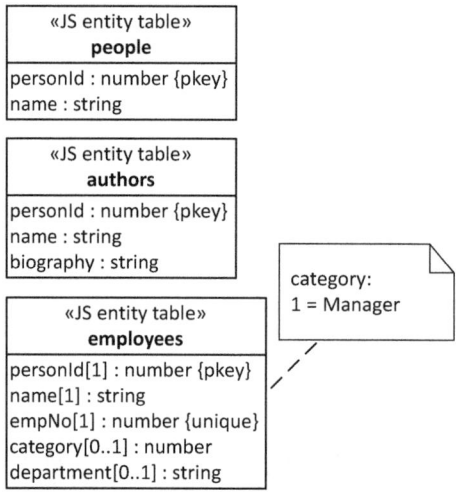

Figure 13.4: A TCI model of the `Person` roles class hierarchy.

In the case of using the JTI approach, in addition to the steps 1–5 above, we would

1. Copy the primary key column (`personId`) of the root table (`people`) to all subtables (`authors` and `employees`).
2. Replace the generalization arrows with «fkey»-stereotyped dependency arrows (representing *foreign key dependencies*) that are annotated at their source end with the name of the subtable's primary key (here: `personId`).

13.3.3 New Issues

Compared to the model of our first case study, shown in Figure 13.1 above, we have to deal with a number of new issues in the *model code*:

1. Defining the subclass relationships between Employee and Person, as well as between Author and Person, using the JS keyword extends discussed in Section 13.1.
2. When loading the instances of the root class (Person.instances) from persistent storage (in Person.retrieveAll), we load (1) the records of the table representing the root class (people) for creating its direct instances and (2) also the records of all other tables representing its subclasses (authors and employees) for creating their direct instances, while also adding their object references to the root class population (to Person.instances). In this way, the root class population does not only contain direct instances, but all instances.
3. When saving the instances of Employee and Author as records of the JS entity tables employees and authors to persistent storage in Employee.saveAll and Author.saveAll (invoked in pl.v.employees.manage.exit and pl.v.authors.manage.exit), we also save the direct instances of Person as records of the people table.

13.3.4 Code the Model Classes of the JS Class Model

The JS class model shown in Figure 13.2 above can be directly coded for getting the code of the model classes Person, Employee and Author as well as for the enumeration type EmployeeCategoryEL.

13.3.4.1 Defining Subtype Relationships

We define the subtype relationships between Employee and Person, as well as between Author and Person, with extends. For instance, in m/Employee.js we define:

```
EmployeeCategoryEL = new Enumeration(["Manager"]);

class Employee extends Person {
  constructor ({personId, name, empNo, category, department}) {
    super({personId, name});
    this.empNo = empNo;
    if (category) this.category = category;
    if (department) this.department = department;
  }
  . . .
}
```

13.3.4.2 Loading the Instances of the Root Class Person

When retrieving the instances of a class hierarchy's root class (in our example, Person) from a persistent data store organized according to the TCI approach, we have to retrieve not only its direct instances from the table representing the root class (people), but also all indirect instances from all tables representing its subclasses (employees and authors), as shown in the following code:

```
Person.retrieveAll = function () {
    var people={}, employees={}, authors={};
    if (!localStorage["authors"]) localStorage["authors"] = "{}";
    if (!localStorage["employees"]) localStorage["employees"] = "{}";
    if (!localStorage["people"]) localStorage["people"] = "{}";
    try {
        people = JSON.parse( localStorage["people"]);
        employees = JSON.parse( localStorage["employees"]);
        authors = JSON.parse( localStorage["authors"]);
    } catch (e) {
        console.log("Error when reading from Local Storage\n" + e);
    }
    for (let key of Object.keys( authors)) {
        try { // convert record to (typed) object
        Author.instances[key] = new Author( authors[key]);
        // create superclass extension
        Person.instances[key] = Author.instances[key];
        } catch (e) {
        console.log(`${e.constructor.name} while deserializing` +
            `author ${key}: ${e.message}`);
    }
    }
    . . .
}
```

Each record of the authors table is retrieved and converted to an Author object, a reference to which is copied to Person.instances. Also the records of the employees table are processed in this way, while the records of the people table are simply retrieved and converted to Person objects:

```
Person.retrieveAll = function () {
    . . .
    for (let key of Object.keys( employees)) {
        . . .
    }
}
```

```
  for (let key of Object.keys( people)) {
    try { // convert record to (typed) object
    Person.instances[key] = new Person( people[key]);
    } catch (e) {
    console.log(`${e.constructor.name} while deserializing` +
        `author ${key}: ${e.message}`);
  }
 }
}
```

13.3.4.3 Saving the Supertable when Saving a Subtable

Since the app's data is kept in main memory as long as the app is running (which is as long as the app's webpage is kept open in the browser), the data has to be saved to persistent storage when the app is exited (e.g., by closing its browser tab), When saving the instances of Employee and Author (as records of the JS entity tables employees and authors) to persistent storage in pl.v.employees.manage.exit and pl.v.authors.manage.exit, we also save the direct instances of Person (as records of the people table). This is necessary because changes to Employee or Author instances may imply changes of Person.instances.

For instance, for Employee data management, we define in v/employees.js:

```
pl.v.employees.manage = {
    . . .
    exit: function () {
    Employee.saveAll();
    Person.saveAll ();
    },
    . . .
}
```

14 Subtyping with Java EE

In this chapter, we explain two case studies based on fragments of the information model of our running example, the *Public Library* app. In the first case study, we consider the single-level class hierarchy with root Book shown in Figure 12.1, which is an incomplete disjoint segmentation. We use the *Single Table Inheritance* approach for mapping this class hierarchy to a single database table.

In the second case study, we consider the multi-level class hierarchy consisting of the Person roles Employee, Manager and Author, shown in Figure 12.8. We use the *Joined Table Inheritance* approach for mapping this class hierarchy to a set of database tables that are related with each other via foreign key dependencies.

In both cases we show
1. how to derive a Java Entity class model,
2. how to code the Java Entity class model in the form of Java Entity classes,
3. how to write the view and controller code based on the model code.

14.1 Subtyping in Java

Java provides built-in support for subtyping with its extends keyword, but it does not support *multiple inheritance*. Consider the following information design model:

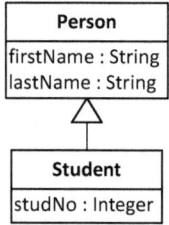

First, we define the superclass Person. Then, we define the subclass Student and its subtype relationship to Person by means of the extends keyword:

```
public class Person {
  private String firstName;
  private String lastName;
  . . .
}
public class Student extends Person {
  private int studentNo;
```

https://doi.org/10.1515/9783110500325-016

```
public Student( String first, String last, int studNo) {
  super( firstName, lastName);
  this.setStudNo( studNo);
 }
 . . .
}
```

Notice that in the Student class, we define a constructor with all the parameters required to create an instance of Student. In this subclass constructor we use super to invoke the constructor of the superclass Person.

14.2 Case Study 1: Implement a Class Hierarchy with *Single Table Inheritance*

In this example we implement the Book hierarchy shown in Figure 12.1. The Java *Entity class model* is derived from this design model.

14.2.1 Make the Java Entity Class Model

Recall that we obtain a Java Entity class modelfrom an OO class model by (1) making all properties private, (2) using Java datatype classes, (3) adding public getters and setters, (4) adding a toString function, (5) adding the (static) data storage methods create, retrieve, update and delete, resulting in the model shown in Figure 14.1.

14.2.2 New Issues

We have to deal with a number of new issues:
1. In the *model code* we have to take care of:
    1. Coding the enumeration type (BookCategoryEL) that is used in the UI code for creating a selection list widget that allows choosing the category of book.
    2. Code each class from the Book class hierarchy using suitable JPA annotations for persistent storage in a corresponding database table, like books.
2. In the *UI code* we have to take care of:
    1. Adding a "Special type" column to the display table of the "retrieve/list all books" use case in retrieveAndListAll.xhtml in the folder WebContent/views/books/. A book without a special category will have an empty table

cell, while for all other books their category will be shown in this cell, along with other segment-specific attribute values.

2. Adding a "Special type" select control, and corresponding form fields for all segment properties, in the forms of the "Create book" and "Update book" use cases in create.xhtml and update.xhtml in the folder WebContent/views/books/. Segment property form fields are only displayed, and their validation is performed, when a corresponding book category has been selected. Such an approach of rendering specific form fields only on certain conditions is sometimes called *dynamic forms*.

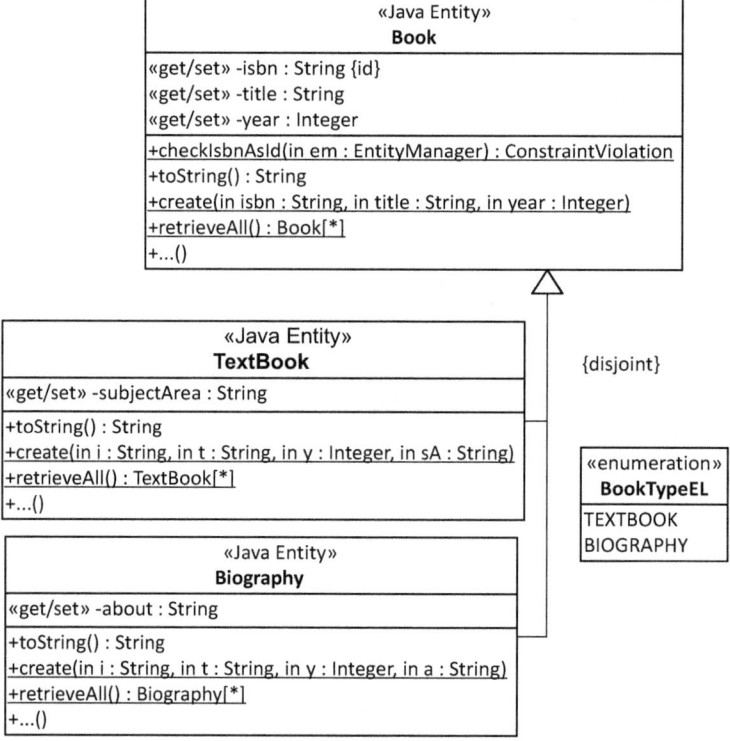

Figure 14.1: The Java Entity class model of the Book class hierarchy.

14.2.3 Code the Classes of the Java Entity Class Model

The Java Entity class model can be directly coded for getting the code of the model classes of our Java EE back-end app.

14.2.3.1 Summary

1. Code the enumeration type (to be used in the facelets) .
2. Code the model classes and add the corresponding JPA annotations for class hierarchy.

These steps are discussed in more detail in the following sections.

14.2.3.2 Code the Enumeration Type BookCategoryEL

The enumeration type BookCategoryEL is coded as a Java enum, providing both enumeration literals as well as (human-readable) labels:

```
public enum BookCategoryEL {
  TEXTBOOK("TextBook"), BIOGRAPHY("Biography");
  private final String label;

  private BookCategoryEL( String label) {
    this.label = label;
  }
  public String getLabel() {return this.label;}
}
```

14.2.3.2.1 Code the Model Classes

We code the model classes Book, TextBook and Biography in the form of Java Entity classes using suitable JPA annotations:

```
@Entity @Table( name="books")
@Inheritance( strategy=InheritanceType.SINGLE_TABLE)
@DiscriminatorColumn( name="category",
    discriminatorType=DiscriminatorType.STRING, length=16)
@DiscriminatorValue( value="BOOK")
@ManagedBean( name="book") @ViewScoped
public class Book {
    @Id @Column( length=10)
    @NotNull( message="An ISBN is required!")
    @Pattern( regexp="\\b\\d{9}(\\d|X)\\b",
        message="The ISBN must be a . . .!")
    private String isbn;
    @Column( nullable=false) @NotNull( message="A title is required!")
    private String title;
    @Column( nullable=false) @NotNull( message="A year is required!")
    @UpToNextYear
```

```
@Min( value=1459, message="The year must not be before 1459!")
private Integer year;
// constructors, set, get and other methods
  . . .
}
```

When using the JPA Single Table Inheritance technique for a class hierarchy, the @Inheritance annotation must be set for the superclass (e.g, Book in our example). It provides the strategy parameter with the value InheritanceType.SINGLE_TABLE. The @DiscriminatorColumn annotation specifies the name of the table column storing the values that discriminate between different types of subclasses (TextBook and Biography, in our example).

Unfortunately, we cannot use our BookCategoryEL enumeration for defining the type of the discriminator column, because Java expressions like BookCategoryEL. TEXTBOOK.name() are not constant, so a Java compiler exception is thrown. Instead, we use DiscriminatorType.STRING. The @DiscriminatorValue annotation specifies a unique value to be stored in the discriminator column of table rows representing an instance of the given class.

Further, we define the subtypes TextBook and Biography:

```
@Entity @Table( name="textbooks")
@DiscriminatorValue( value="TEXTBOOK")
@ManagedBean( name="textBook") @ViewScoped
public class TextBook extends Book {
    @Column( nullable=false) @NotNull(
        message="A subject area value is required")
    String subjectArea;
    // constructors, set, get and other methods
    . . .
}
```

TextBook and Biography are subclasses of Book, so we define them with extends Book. For each subclass, we add a @DiscriminatorValue annotation with a value from the BookCategoryEL enumeration.

14.2.4 STI Database Schema

As a result of the annotation

```
@Inheritance( strategy=InheritanceType.SINGLE_TABLE)
```

only one database table is used for representing a class hierarchy. This table contains the columns corresponding to all the properties of all the classes from the hierarchy plus the discriminator column. In our example, the books table contains the following columns: isbn, title, year, subjectArea, about and category. The simplified corresponding SQL-DDL code internally used to generate the books table for our application is shown below:

```
CREATE TABLE IF NOT EXISTS `books` (
    `ISBN` varchar(10) NOT NULL,
    `TITLE` varchar(255) NOT NULL,
    `YEAR` int(11) NOT NULL,
    `SUBJECTAREA` varchar(255) DEFAULT NULL,
    `ABOUT` varchar(255) DEFAULT NULL,
    `category` varchar(16) DEFAULT NULL,
)
```

14.2.5 Write the View And Controller Code

The user interface (UI) consists of a start page that allows navigating to the data management pages (in our example, to index.xhtml in the folder WebContent/ views/books/). Such a data management page contains four sections: *retrieve/list all books*, *create book*, *update book* and *delete book*.

14.2.5.1 Summary
We have to take care of handling the category discriminator and the subjectArea and about segment properties both in the "List all books" use case as well as in the "Create book" and "Update book" use cases by

1. Adding a segment information column ("Special type") to the display table of the *Retrieve/List All* use case in retrieveAndListAll.xhtml in the folder WebContent/views/books/.
2. Adding a "Special type" select control, and corresponding form fields for all segment properties, in the forms of the "Create book" and "Update book" use cases in create.xhtml and update.xhtml in the folder WebContent/views/ books/. Segment property form fields are only displayed, and their validation occurs only when a corresponding book category has been selected.

14.2.5.2 Add a Segment Information Column in *Retrieve/List All*

We add a "Special type" column to the display table of the "List all books" use case in books.html:

```
<h:dataTable value="#{bookController.books}" var="b">
  . . .
  <h:column>
    <f:facet name="header">Special type</f:facet>
    #{b.getClass().getSimpleName() != 'Book' ?
        b.getClass().getSimpleName() : ''}
  </h:column>
</h:dataTable>
```

A conditional expression is used to check if the Java bean class name is Book, in which case we don't show it, or if it is something else (e.g. TextBook or Biography), and then it is shown. This expression also shows how you can call/use various Java bean methods, not only custom methods.

14.2.5.3 Add a "Special Type" Select Control in *Create* and *Update*

In both use cases, we need to allow selecting a special category of book ('textbook' or 'biography') with the help of a select control in a *panel grid* element:

```
<h:panelGrid id="bookPanel" columns="3">
  . . .
  <h:outputText value="Special type: " />
  <h:selectOneMenu id="bookType" value="#{viewScope.bookTypeVal}">
    <f:selectItem itemLabel="---"/>
    <f:selectItems value="#{book.typeItems}" />
    <f:ajax event="change" execute="@this"    render="textBookPanel
        biographyBookPanel standardBookPanel"/>
  </h:selectOneMenu>
  <h:message for="bookType" errorClass="error" />
</h:panelGrid>
```

In the select control, three alternative *panel groups* are referenced:
1. A "standardBookPanel":

```
<h:panelGroup id="standardBookPanel">
  <h:commandButton value="Create"
      rendered="#{viewScope.bookTypeVal == null}"
      action="#{bookController.create( book.isbn,
```

```
        book.title, book.year)}" />
</h:panelGroup>
```

2. A "textBookPanel":

```
<h:panelGroup id="textBookPanel">
  <h:panelGrid rendered="#{viewScope.bookTypeVal == 'TEXTBOOK'}"
        columns="3">
    <h:outputText value="Subject area: " />
    <h:inputText id="subjectArea" value="#{textBook.subjectArea}"/>
    <h:message for="subjectArea" errorClass="error" />
  </h:panelGrid>
  <h:commandButton value="Create"
        rendered="#{viewScope.bookTypeVal == 'TEXTBOOK'}"
        action="#{textBookController.create( book.isbn, book.title,
            book.year, textBook.subjectArea)}" />
</h:panelGroup>
```

3. A "biographyBookPanel":

```
<h:panelGroup id="biographyBookPanel">
  <h:panelGrid rendered="#{viewScope.bookTypeVal == 'BIOGRAPHY'}"
        columns="3">
    <h:outputText value="About: " />
    <h:inputText id="about" value="#{biographyBook.about}"/>
    <h:message for="about" errorClass="error" />
  </h:panelGrid>
  <h:commandButton value="Create"
        rendered="#{viewScope.bookTypeVal == 'BIOGRAPHY'}"
        action="#{biographyBookController.create( book.isbn,
            book.title, book.year, biographyBook.about)}" />
</h:panelGroup>
```

There are a few important remarks on the above code:
- the h:selectOneMenu is used to create a single selection list which is populated with book titles by using the getTypeItems method of the Book class. A more detailed explanation is presented in Part 3 enumeration app.
- it is possible to conditionally render facelet components by using the rendered attribute. The JSF EL expression must return true or false, this making the HTML resulting elements to be part of the HTML DOM or not. Notice that the conditional expressions are evaluated in the server side. This is the method we use to hide or show the input form elements corresponding to various book

types (e.g., TextBook has a subjectArea property while Biography has an about property).

- the render attribute used with f:ajax specifies which of the JSF components are to be updated . This is needed because of the live DOM changes (client side, not server side) which applies after the AJAX call.
- AJAX is used to submit the form for reevaluation when the special type selection list field is changed (something is selected). As a result, it enforces the rendering of the three panels corresponding to three book cases: simple book, text book and biography. Using execute="@this" we enforce the re-evaluation of the form at server side, so the resulting HTML DOM structure contains the changes accordiong to the conditions specified by the rendered attributes of the various JSF elements. Notice that a JSF element that has a conditional rendered expression must be a child of another JSF element which is always part of the DOM.
- h:panelGroup is used to define a set of elements which are either shown or hidden.
- the action attribute of the h:commandButton can't be used with conditional expressions, therefore we have to create three command buttons, one for each case: create/update a Book, a TextBook or a Biography. The create method of the corresponding controller class (i.e., BookController, TextBookController or BiographyController is called).
- since we do not have a corresponding property in the Java bean class(es) for the special type (category), we can use JSF variables to store the value of the single select list, and then use the variable in rendered conditions for various elements. Therefore, for the h:selectOneMenu, the value="#{viewScope.bookTypeVal}" specifies that we use a "on the fly" defined property named bookTypeVal, which is part of the view scope internal JSF object(s). We can also define such variable outside the view scope, e.g., value="#{bookTypeVal}", but in this case they are request scoped, so their value is lost after submitting the form, and the rendered conditions can't be correctly evaluated.

For a class in the class hierarchy, one corresponding controller class is defined. It contains the specific create, update and delete methods. The shared methods, such as getAllObjects are defined by the controller of the top level class (e.g., for our example, this is BookController). See minimal app for more details on how to implement the controller class and the corresponding CRUD methods.

The *Update Book* test case is very similar with the *Create Book* test case. The *Delete Book* test case remains unchanged.

14.3 Case Study 2: Implement a Class Hierarchy with *Joined Table Inheritance*

The starting point for our case study is the design model shown in Figure 12.8 above. In the following sections, we show how to eliminate the Manager class by using the *Class Hierarchy Merge* design pattern and how to implement the Person hierarchy and use *Joined, Multiple Table Inheritance* storage with the help of JPA framework.

14.3.1 Make the Java Entity class model

We design the *model classes* of our example app with the help of a Java *Entity class model* that we derive from the *design model* by essentially leaving the generalization arrows as they are and just adding *getters* and *setters* to each class. However, in the case of our example app, it is natural to apply the *Class Hierarchy Merge* design pattern to the segmentation of Employee for simplifying the data model by eliminating the Manager subclass. This leads to the model shown in Figure 14.2 below. Notice that we have also made two technical design decisions:

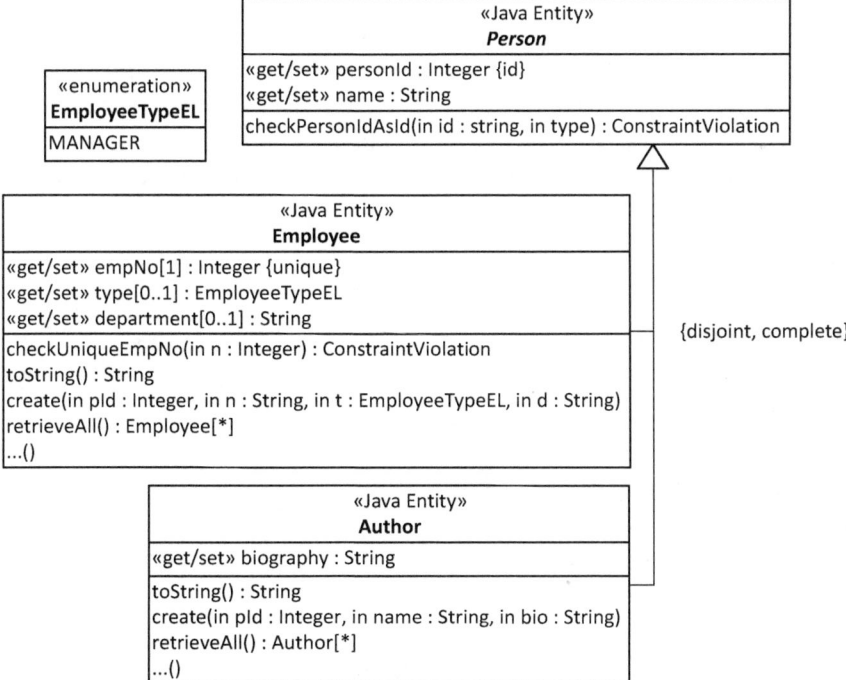

Figure 14.2: The Java Entity class model of the Person class hierarchy.

1. We have declared the segmentation of Person into Employee and Author to be *disjoint* and *complete*, that is, any person is either an employee or an author. Since Java does not *support multiple classification*, we cannot implement an overlapping segmentation, as needed when modeling roles, with Java.

2. We have turned Person into an ***abstract class*** (indicated by its name written in italics in the class rectangle), which means that it cannot have direct instances, but only indirect ones via its subclasses Employee and Author. This technical design decision is compatible with the fact that any Person is an Employee or an Author (or both), and consequently there is no need for any object to instantiate Person directly.

14.3.2 New Issues

Compared to the model of our first case study, shown in Figure 14.1 above, we have to define the category relationships between Employee and Person, as well as between Author and Person, using the JPA annotation.

In the *UI code* we have to take care of:

1. Adding the views (in the folders WebContent/views/authors and WebContent/views/employees) and controller classes (AuthorController and EmployeeController) for the corresponding Author and Employee model classes.

2. Deal with the Manager case, by adding a "Special type" select control, in the forms of the "Create book" and "Update book" use cases in WebContent/views/books/create.xhtml and WebContent/views/books/update.xhtml. Segment property form fields (i.e., department in our example) are only displayed, and their validation is performed, when a corresponding employee type has been selected.

14.3.3 Code the Model Classes of the Java Entity Class Model

The Java Entity class model shown in Figure 14.2 above is coded by using the JavaBeans Person, Employee and Author as well as for the enumeration type EmployeeCategoryEL.

14.3.3.1 Define the Category Relationships
We define the category relationships between Employee and Person, as well as between Author and Person, using the JPA annotations. At first we create the Person class as shown below:

```
@Entity @Table(name="persons")
@Inheritance(strategy=InheritanceType.JOINED)
```

```
@DiscriminatorColumn(name="category",
    discriminatorType=DiscriminatorType.STRING, length=16)
public abstract class Person {
    @Id @NotNull(message="A person ID is required!")
    private Integer personId;
    @NotNull(message="A name is required!") @Column(nullable=false)
    private String name;
    . . .
}
```

Comparing with the Book hierarchy shown in *Test Case 1*, the @Inheritance annotations defines now the strategy=InheritanceType.JOINED. This means, for every class in the inheritance hierarchy, a database table is used. The @DiscriminatorColumn (name="category") specifies the column in the corresponding table (i.e., persons) of the top hierarchy class (i.e., Person) which stores the discriminator values used to identify the stored type of each entry (table row).

Notice that the Java class Person is declared as being abstract, which means it can't be initialized, instead we can and we initialize subclasses derived from it (i.e., Employee and Author). This also mean that we don't declare a @DiscriminatorValue because no direct instance of Person is stored in the database table.

Further, we define the Author class as follows:

```
@Entity @Table(name="authors")
@DiscriminatorValue( value="AUTHOR")
@ManagedBean(name="author") @ViewScoped
public class Author extends Person {
    @NotNull(message="A biography is required!")
    private String biography;
    . . .
}
```

The Author class inherits Person, therefore the get and set methods corresponding to personId and name properties are available. The @DiscriminatorValue(value="AUTHOR") specifies that the column category of the persons table stores the value AUTHOR for every entry which comes from persisting an Author instance.

Finally, we define the Employee class:

```
@Entity @Table(name="employees")
@DiscriminatorValue(value="EMPLOYEE")
@ManagedBean(name="employee") @ViewScoped
public class Employee extends Person {
    @Column( nullable=false)
```

```
@NotNull( message="An employee ID is required!")
private Integer empNo;
@Column( nullable=false, length=32)
@Enumerated( EnumType.STRING)
private EmployeeCategoryEL type;
@Column( nullable=true, length=64)
private String department;
. . .
}
```

Notice the type property used to identify the Employee type, such as Manager. Its values are defined by the EmployeeCategoryEL enumeration.

14.3.3.2 Database Schema for Joined Table Class Hierarchy
As a result of the annotation

```
@Inheritance( strategy = InheritanceType.JOINED)
```

for each class in the inheritance hierarchy, one database table is created. The corresponding simplified SQL-DDL scripts used by JPA to create the persons, authors and employees tables are shown below:

```
CREATE TABLE IF NOT EXISTS `persons` (
    `PERSONID` int(11) NOT NULL,
    `category` varchar(16) DEFAULT NULL,
    `NAME` varchar(255) NOT NULL
);
CREATE TABLE IF NOT EXISTS `authors` (
    `PERSONID` int(11) NOT NULL,
    `BIOGRAPHY` varchar(255) DEFAULT NULL
);
ADD CONSTRAINT `FK_authors_PERSONID` FOREIGN KEY (`PERSONID`)
    REFERENCES `persons` (`PERSONID`);
CREATE TABLE IF NOT EXISTS `employees` (
    `PERSONID` int(11) NOT NULL,
    `DEPARTMENT` varchar(64) DEFAULT NULL,
    `EMPNO` int(11) NOT NULL,
    `TYPE` varchar(32) DEFAULT NULL
);
ADD CONSTRAINT `FK_employees_PERSONID` FOREIGN KEY (`PERSONID`)
    REFERENCES `persons` (`PERSONID`);
```

As we can see, every table contains the direct properties as defined by the corresponding Java bean class. Additionally, the authors and employees tables are created with a foreign key constraing for the PERSONID column refering to to the PERSONID column from the persons table.

14.3.4 Write the View and Controller Code

In the user interface, for every Java bean class, we have a controller class which contains the create, update and delete CRUD methods. The PersonController class is defined as abstract and contains the checkPersonIdAsId method, which is common to all subclasses. The AuthorController and EmployeeController inherits the PersonController.

For every non-abstract entity class in the inheritance hierarchy we define a set of views corresponding to CRUD operations. For example, in the case of Author we have the files retrieveAndListAll.xhtml, create.xhtml, update.xhtml, and delete.xhtml in the folder WebContent/views/authors/. In the case of Employee, the *Retrieve/List All Employees* use case requires to display the *Special type of employee* column:

```
<h:column>
 <f:facet name="header">Special type of employee</f:facet>
 #{e.type != null ? e.type.label.concat(" of ").concat(
                 e.department).concat(" department") : ""}
</h:column>
```

Notice that within EL expressions we cannot use the + (plus) operator for concatenating strings. EL allows the + operator to be used only for numeric addition. However, we can use the concat method instead.

14.4 Run the App

For running your application, you may first have to stop your Tomcat/TomEE server (with bin/shutdown.bat for Windows or bin/shutdown.sh for Linux). Next, download and unzip our ZIP archive file containing all the source code of the application and also the ANT script file that you have to edit (modify the server.folder property value). Now, execute the following command in your console or terminal:

```
ant deploy -Dappname=SubtypingApp
```

Finally, start your Tomcat web server (by using `bin/startup.bat` for Windows OS or `bin/startup.sh` for Linux). Please be patient, this can take some time depending on the speed of your computer. It will be ready when the console displays the following message: *INFO: Initializing Mojarra [some library versions and paths are shonw here] for context '/subtypingapp'*. Finally, open a web browser and type:

```
http://localhost:8080/SubtypingApp/WebContent/views/app/index.xhtml
```

15 Subtyping Practice Projects

15.1 Project 1 – Person Types and Movie Types

The purpose of the app to be built is managing information about movies as well as
their directors and actors whwre two types of movies are distinguished: biographies
and episodes of TV series, as shown in the following model:

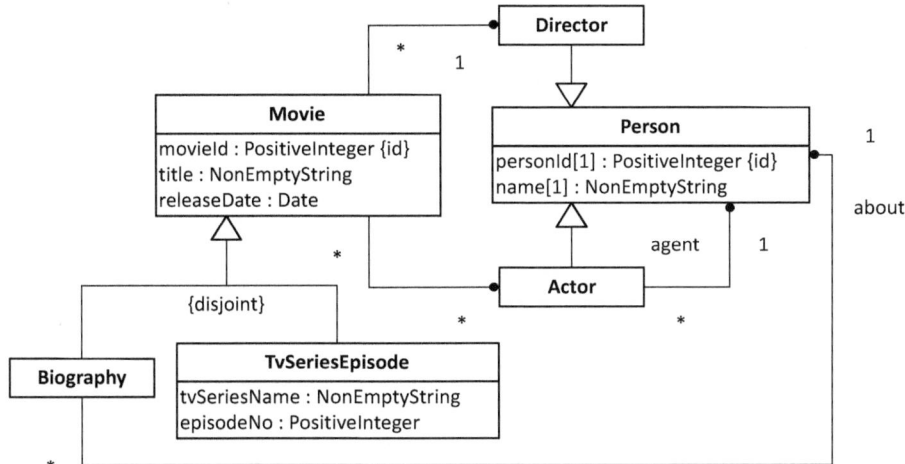

Code the app by following our guidelines.

Make sure that your pages comply with the XML syntax of HTML5, and that your
JavaScript code complies with our Coding Guidelines (and is checked with JSHint).

https://doi.org/10.1515/9783110500325-017

Glossary

C

CRUD	CRUD is an acronym for *Create*, *Read/Retrieve*, *Update*, *Delete*, which denote the four basic data management operations to be performed by any software application.
Cascading Style Sheets	CSS is used for defining the presentation style of web pages by telling the browser how to render their HTML (or XML) contents: using which layout of content elements, which fonts and text styles, which colors, which backgrounds, and which animations. Normally, these settings are made in a separate CSS file that is associated with an HTML file via a special link element in the HTML's head element.

D

Document Object Model)	The DOM is an abstract API for retrieving and modifying nodes and elements of HTML or XML documents. All web programming languages have DOM bindings that realize the DOM.
Domain Name System	The DNS translates user-friendly domain names to IP addresses that allow to locate a host computer on the Internet.

E

ECMAScript	A standard for JavaScript defined by the industry organization "Ecma International".
Extensible Markup Language	XML allows to mark up the structure of all kinds of documents, data files and messages in a machine-readable way. XML may also be human-readable, if the tag names used are self-explaining. XML is based on Unicode. SVG and MathML are based on XML, and there is an XML-based version of HTML. XML provides a syntax for expressing structured information in the form of an *XML document* with *elements* and their *attributes*. The specific elements and attributes used in an XML document can come from any vocabulary, such as public standards or user-defined XML formats.

https://doi.org/10.1515/9783110500325-018

H

Hypertext Markup Language	HTML allows marking up (or describing) the structure of a human-readable web document or web user interface. The XML-based version of HTML, which is called "XHTML5", provides a simpler and cleaner syntax compared to traditional HTML.
Hypertext Transfer Protocol	HTTP is a stateless request/response protocol based on the Internet technologies TCP/IP and DNS, using human-readable text messages for the communication between web clients and web servers. The main purpose of HTTP has been to allow fetching web documents identified by URLs from a web browser, and invoking the operations of a back-end web application program from an HTML form executed by a web browser. More recently, HTTP is increasingly used for providing web APIs and web services.

I

IANA	IANA stands for *Internet Assigned Numbers Authority*, which is a subsidiary of ICANN responsible for names and numbers used by Internet protocols.
ICANN	ICANN stands for *Internet Corporation of Assigned Names and Numbers*, which is an international nonprofit organization that maintains the domain name system.
IndexedDB	A JavaScript API for indexed data storage managed by browsers. Indexing allows high-performance searching. Like many SQL DBMS, IndexedDB supports database transactions.
I18N	A set of best practices that help to adapt products to any target language and culture. It deals with multiple character sets, units of measure, keyboard layouts, time and date formats, and text directions.

J

JSON	JSON stands for *JavaScript Object Notation*, which is a data-interchange format following the JavaScript syntax for object literals. Many programming languages support JSON as a light-weight alternative to XML.

M

MathML	An open standard for representing mathematical expressions, either in data interchange or for rendering them within webpages.
MIME	A MIME type (also called "media type" or "content type") is a keyword string sent along with a file for indicating its content type. For example, a sound file might be labeled `audio/ogg`, or an image file `image/png`.
Model-View-Controller	MVC is a general architecture metaphor emphasizing the principle of separation of concerns, mainly between the model and the view, and considering the model as the most fundamental part of an app. In MVC frameworks, "M", "V" and "C" are defined in different ways. Often the term "model" refers to the app's data sources, while the "view" denotes the app's code for the user interface, which is based on CSS-styled HTML forms and DOM events, and the "controller" typically denotes the (glue) code that is in charge of mediating between the *view* and the *model*.

O

Object Constraint Language	The OCL is a formal logic language for expressing integrity constraints, mainly in UML class models. It also allows defining derivation expressions for defining derived properties, and defining preconditions and postconditions for operations, in a class model.
Object-Oriented Programming	OOP is a programming paradigm based on the concepts of *objects* and *classes* instantiated by objects. Classes are like blueprints for objects: they define their *properties* and the *methods/functions* that can be applied to them. A higher-level characteristic of OOP is *inheritance* in class hierarchies: a subclass inherits the features (properties, methods and constraints) of its superclass.

Web Ontology Language	OWL is formal logic language for knowledge representation on the Web. It allows defining vocabularies (mainly classes with properties) and supports expressing many types of integrity constraints on them. OWL is the basis for performing automated inferences, such as checking the consistency of an OWL vocabulary. Vocabularies, or data models, defined in the form of UML class models can be converted to OWL vocabularies and then checked for consistency.

P

Portable Network Graphics	PNG is an open (non-proprietary) graphics file format that supports lossless data compression.
Polyfill	A polyfill is a piece of JavaScript code for emulating a standard JavaScript method in a browser, which does not support the method.

R

Resource Description Framework	RDF is a W3C language for representing machine-readable propositional information on the Web.

S

Standard Generalized Markup Language	SGML is an ISO specification for defining markup languages. HTML4 has been defined with SGML. XML is a simplified successor of SGML. HTML5 is no longer SGML-based and has its own parsing rules.
Scalable Vector Graphics	SVG is a 2D vector image format based on XML. SVG can be styled with CSS and made interactive using JavaScript. HTML5 allows direct embedding of SVG content in an HTML document.
Slot	A slot is a name-value pair. In an object of an object-oriented program (for instance, in a Java object), a slot normally is a property-value pair. But in a JavaScript object, a slot may also consist of a method name and a method body or it may be a key-value pair of a map.

U

Unicode	A platform-independent character set that includes almost all characters from most of the world's script languages including Hindi, Burmese and Gaelic. Each character is assigned a unique integer code in the range between 0 and 1,114,111. For example, the Greek letter π has the code 960. Unicode includes legacy character sets like ASCII and ISO-8859-1 (Latin-1) as subsets.
	XML is based on Unicode. Consequently, the Greek letter π (with code 960) can be inserted in an XML document as π using the XML entity syntax. The default encoding of Unicode characters in an XML document is UTF-8, which uses only a single byte for ASCII characters, but three bytes for less common characters.
Uniform Resource Identifier	A URI is either a *Uniform Resource Locator (URL)* or a *Uniform Resource Name (URN)*.
Uniform Resource Locator	A URL is a resource name that contains a web address for locating the resource on the Web.
Unified Modeling Language	The UML is an industry standard that defines a set of modeling languages for making various kinds of models and diagrams in support of object-oriented problem analysis and software design. Its core languages are *Class Diagrams* for information/data modeling, and *Sequence Diagrams*, *Activity Diagrams* and *State Diagrams* (or *State Charts*) for process/behavior modeling.
Uniform Resource Name	A URN refers to a resource without specifying its location.
User Agent	A user agent is a front-end web client program such as a web browser.

W

WebM	WebM is an open (royalty-free) web video format supported by Google Chrome and Mozilla Firefox, but not by Microsoft Internet Explorer and Apple Safari.
Web Hypertext Application Technology Working Group	The *WHATWG* was established in 2004 by former employees of Apple, Mozilla, and Opera who have been unhappy with the slow progress of web technology standardization due to W3C's choice to focus on the standardization of XHTML2. Led by Ian Hickson, they developed HTML5 and related JavaScript APIs in competition and collaboration with the W3C.

World Wide Web	The WWW (or, simply, "the Web") is a huge client-server network based on HTTP, HTML and XML, where web browsers (and other 'user agents'), acting as HTTP clients, access web server programs, acting as HTTP servers.
World Wide Web Consortium	The *W3C* is an international organization in charge of developing and maintaining web standards.

X

XML HTTP Request	The XML HTTP Request (XHR) API allows a JavaScript program to exchange HTTP messages with back-end programs. It can be used for retrieveing/submitting information from/to a back-end program without submitting HTML forms. XHR-based approaches have been subsumed under the acronym "AJAX" in the past.

Index

https://doi.org/10.1515/9783110500325-019